PRAISE FOR *GLOBAL UNIONS, GLOBAL BUSINESS*

'This pathbreaking book provides both an invaluable resource on the history of global union federations, and new insights on current issues and contestations. It will be of great interest to all with an interest in the state of unions worldwide, commentators and critics of globalization, and those concerned with fairness at work in a wide range of contexts.'

Professor Geoffrey Wood, University of Sheffield

'Powerfully argued and impressively documented, this stimulating book provides a readable, insightful introduction to the challenges facing global trade unionism. It will prove of tremendous value to both union activists and academics teaching international business, international employment relations and HRM.'

Professor John McIlroy, Keele University

'This book is an excellent example of public social science. Focused principally on global union federations it is historically informed, empirically rich and argues that the key to international union renewal and success is education (informed by research). I most strongly recommend it.'

Professor Peter Fairbrother, Cardiff University

'Elizabeth Cotton and Richard Croucher have written the essential guide to international trade unionism: its actors, its structure, its history, its functions, its activities. I know of no other recent book that details as clearly what the international trade union movement actually does and why it is important for workers everywhere. Its weaknesses are not glossed over but Cotton and Croucher have proposals on how these can be addressed. A must read for trade unionists and for activists in the global justice and solidarity movement.'

Dan Gallin, Global Labour Institute

GLOBAL UNIONS, GLOBAL BUSINESS

GLOBAL UNIONS, GLOBAL BUSINESS

Global Union Federations and International Business

RICHARD CROUCHER

AND

ELIZABETH COTTON

Middlesex
University
PRESS

First published in 2009 by Middlesex University Press

Copyright © Richard Croucher and Elizabeth Cotton

ISBN 978 1 904750 62 8

A CIP catalogue record for this book is available from The British Library

Cover design by Helen Taylor
Typesetting by Carnegie Publishing Ltd
Printed in the UK by Ashford Colour Press Ltd

Mixed Sources
Product group from well-managed
forests and other controlled sources
www.fsc.org Cert no. SA-COC-1527
© 1996 Forest Stewardship Council
FSC

Middlesex University Press
Fenella Building
The Burroughs
Hendon
London NW4 4BT
Tel: +44 (0)20 8411 4162: +44 (0)20 8411 4161
Fax: +44 (0)20 8411 4167
www.mupress.co.uk

Contents

Preface

THIS book is aimed at all those interested in the experience of working people in the current phase of globalisation. We have incurred debts to many such people in writing it. Experts in international business, corporate social responsibility, international trade unionism and others have generously shared information and their thoughts with us. We therefore thank Mare Anceva, Ross Brennan, Samar Badar Al-Husan, Alexandr Ivakhno, Aranya Pakapath, Cristhian Rivas, Carlos Bustos, Wolfgang Weinz and Fabian Nkomo.

A group of specialists in different aspects of our subject kindly read and commented on an earlier version, and we are grateful to Paul Gooderham, Rebecca Gumbrell-McCormick, John McIlroy, Ingo Singe, David Cockroft and Dan Gallin.

We are especially grateful to Ifan Shepherd, who prepared the maps and diagrams for publication with characteristic good humour and patience, to Jane Tinkler for her help in navigating the LSE library and John Callaghan who kindly edited a late version of the manuscript. Any remaining inaccuracies are the authors' joint responsibility.

Finally, we thank all those trade unionists who have discussed these subjects with us over the years. We hope they will find the book a fair and useful account of their remarkable work.

Richard Croucher
Elizabeth Cotton

List of Tables

List of Diagrams

List of Maps

List of Initialisations and Acronyms

AA	Anglo American plc (Company)
ACFTU	All-China Federation of Trade Unions
AFL-CIO	American Federation of Labour-Congress of Industrial Organizations
AFRO	African Regional Organisation (of the ITUC)
AGA	Anglo Gold Ashanti (Company)
ART	Antiretroviral Therapy
ARV	Antiretrovirals
BASF	Badische Anilin und Soda Fabrik (company)
BWI	Building and Wood Workers' International
CGIL	Confederazione Generale Italiana del Lavoro (Italian Confederation of Trade Unions)
CGT	Confédération Générale du Travail (French Confederation of Trade Unions)
CIS	Commonwealth of Independent States
CSR	Corporate Social Responsibility
CTA	Central de Trabajadores Argentinos (Argentinian National Centre)
CUT	Central Unitaria de Trabajadores (Colombian National Union Centre)
EI	Educational International
EPZ	Export Processing Zone
ETUC	European Trade Union Confederation
EWC	European Works Council
FDI	Foreign direct investment
FES	Friedrich Ebert Stiftung (German Friedrich Ebert Foundation)
FNPR	Federatsiia Nevasymykh Profsoiuzov Rossii (Federation of Russian Trade Unions)
FNV	Federatie Nederlandse Vakbeweging (Dutch Confederation of Trade Unions)
FOC	Flags of Convenience
GATT	General Agreement on Tariffs and Trade
GBC	Global Business Coalition
GFA	Global Framework Agreement
GMWU	Ghana Mineworkers' Union

GUF	Global Union Federation
GURN	Global Unions Research Network
HRM	Human resource management
ICEF	International Federation of Chemical, Energy and General Workers' Unions (1946–1995)
ICEM	International Federation of Chemical, Energy, Mine and General Workers' Unions (1995–)
ICFTU	International Confederation of Free Trade Unions
IFA	International Framework Agreement
IFBWW	International Federation of Building and Woodworkers
IFCTU	International Federation of Christian Trade Unions
IFJ	International Federation of Journalists
IFTU	International Federation of Trade Unions
ILO	International Labour Office/Organization
IMF	International Metalworkers' Federation
ISF	International Shipping Federation
ISNTUC	International Secretariat of National Trade Union Centres
ITF	International Transport Workers' Federation
ITGLWF	International Textile, Garment and Leather Workers' Federation
ITS	International Trade Secretariat
ITUC	International Trade Union Confederation
IUF	International Union of Food, Agricultural, Hotel, Restaurant, Catering, Tobacco and Allied Workers' Associations
IWMA	International Working Men's Association
LO Norway	Landsorganisasjonen i Norge (Norwegian Confederation of Trade Unions)
LO-FTF	Landsorgasitionen I Danmark/Funktionærernes og Tjenestemændenes Fællesråd, (Danish Confederation of Trade Unions)
LO-TCO	Landsorganisationen i Sverige/ Tjänstemännens Centralorganisation (Swedish Trade Union Confederation)
MNC	Multinational company
NGO	Non-governmental organisation
NUM	National Union of Mineworkers, South Africa (Union)
OECD	Organisation for Economic Co-operation and Development
OGWU	Oil and Gas Workers' Union, Azerbaijan (Union)
OPZZ	Ogolnopolskie Propozumienie Zwiazkow Zawodowych, Poland (All Poland Alliance of Trade Unions)
PCFT	Petrol and Chemical Federation of Thailand (Union)
PSI	Public Services International
RILU	Red International of Labour Unions

ROGWU	Russian Oil and Gas Workers' Union
SASK	Suomen Ammattiliittojen Solidaarsuuskeskus (Finnish Trade Union Foundation)
TUC	Trades Union Congress, UK
UNCTAD	United Nations Conference on Trade and Development
UNDP	United Nations Development Programme
UNI	Union Network International
USWA	United Steel Workers of America (Union)
VCT	Voluntary counselling and testing
VWWC	Volkswagen World Works Council
WCL	World Confederation of Labour
WFTU	World Federation of Trade Unions

I
Contexts

CHAPTER ONE

Introduction

We had been approached by phone calls from some crew members of the vessel *Little Kid-II*, a Cambodian-flagged ship, saying that they were not being paid. We spoke several times to the Ship Manager insisting that they pay all the money due to the seafarers. The company totally ignored its obligations to the crew and did not pay them when they were due, even though the rate they were paid was below the International Transport Workers' Federation (ITF) rate.

On 20th of December 2006 we were informed by the seafarers that the vessel was calling at Rostov-on-Don (Russia). We asked for the help of the ITF Actions and Claims Unit in London, and following their detailed advice contacted their Russian colleagues. We advised the ITF affiliate, the regional organisation of the Seafarers' Union of Russia (SUR) of the situation, asking for their assistance. At the same time we recommended that the seafarers spoke to SUR, and supplied them with the contact details. We and SUR recommended the crew members to organize protest actions. To help the seafarers in these actions two SUR representatives were sent on board (Mr. Zenkovskiy, head, and Mr. Petchenko).

The port authorities, frontier guards and the company itself were alerted to the coming actions. The guards put obstacles in the union's way. The vessel's captain put pressure on the crew aimed at getting them to abandon their action and promising to pay out the balance of the wages due later, in Istanbul and trying not to permit the union's representatives to come onboard. Later the frontier guards just took back SUR's permissions to enter, but they went on contacting the crew by phone and outside of the port persuading them to go on with the actions.

This, and the knowledge that the ITF was watching the case, inspired the seafarers to continue their sanctions. It took several days, but finally the company gave in when they received evidence that they had no choice but to pay out the wages, and they knew the ITF was involved.

Extract from an interview with Alexandr Ivakhno,
Ukrainian Seafarers' Union, 20 January 2008

This book analyses the work of the Global Union Federations, illustrated in our opening quotation, and makes suggestions for their re-orientation. We discuss the current position of the trade union movement's international institutions, their internal lives and their relations with companies. The book is therefore a contribution to a widely overlooked aspect of globalisation.

Unions remain by far the largest membership organisations in the world and have extensive international coverage, dwarfing non-governmental organisations (NGOs) also engaged with the impact of globalisation. Although NGOs are often regarded more positively than unions, they rarely have membership structures and generally rely on unelected professionals (Edwards, 2001; Batliwala, 2002). In terms of democratic involvement, unions provide much greater opportunities for members to determine policy and play a part in organisational governance. Despite some historic cases internationally of corruption, trade unions have long and proud traditions of democratic processes. They provide a substantial proportion of working people with opportunities for political involvement, and for shifting power relations at work. This aspect of unionism has taken on renewed importance with the development of global trade. Nevertheless, we also argue that without change in the ways that the international institutions of the trade union movement operate, the existing power dynamics will remain intact and globalisation will continue to operate in negative ways for many workers.

Our primary focus is on the global union organisations themselves, significant but little-studied actors in the construction of the beginnings of an international system of industrial relations. The work of these organisations is important in coordinating union responses to longstanding distributive and procedural justice issues that have been exacerbated by globalisation. Real possibilities exist for international trade unionism to build its position within these discussions. The distribution of wealth and access to resources such as health and education within countries is central to current debates around development, and unions are relevant because of their redistributive capacity. As Elliott and Freeman (2003) argue, the 'missing voice' in these debates is that of workers in developing countries. Unionisation has a major contribution to make in rectifying that position. Unions have many positive outcomes for workers, facilitating collective voice mechanisms that help to increase their earnings and reduce earnings differentials, including gender earnings differentials (Freeman and Medoff, 1984; Weichselbaumer and Winter-Ebner, 2003). They help to enforce the law in workplaces (Harcourt et al., 2004). The benefits they bring to society more generally are well established. Unions internationally gave birth to many other cooperative, mutual and adult educational organisations, building civil society and promoting 'democratic development' (Stiglitz, 2000). Stiglitz linked this to the way that unions have historically played a major role in providing opportunities for democratic involvement, including by addressing workers' needs to improve their wider understandings through education.

Many international companies are involved in a quest to show that they have 'fair' labour practices without recognising unions. These quests involve increasingly elaborate and ineffective methods of monitoring themselves and their suppliers, for example by finding NGOs that will attest to the humanity of their practices through inspection processes and so on. It then appears to be a matter of surprise to them that there is a persistent pattern of rediscovery by investigative journalists showing that in fact these problems have not been resolved. The harsh reality is that for many of the world's workers, talk of human rights in the workplace is just that: it is strictly rhetorical (Douzinas, 2000; Beirnaert, 2008). It is evident that only stable union organisation within workplaces can begin to deal with both rights and distributive issues on an ongoing basis; no monitoring or inspection system can hope to match such organisation.

Our subject is important precisely because of trade unionism's widespread decline. The fall in union membership in most countries is caused primarily by objective circumstances: massive restructuring in global capitalism that has hugely disrupted well-unionised industries and created weak negotiating positions for workers. Both have of course been facilitated by the rise and dominance of neoliberal ideas.

Unions' difficulties are inextricably linked with the problems faced by workers across the world. Labour's share of total income has been falling in the developed countries for some years. In the UK, labour took a rising share of national income for the century up to 1970, but this trend has now been reversed (Glyn, 2006). This is not only because of the expanded world labour supply; it is also partly because of relatively low levels of investment. Further reasons are found in: the new international division of labour; the ever present threat of relocation; the development of different forms of human resource management; the widespread adoption of Japanese production models; lean production; 'High Performance Work Systems'; and the pursuit of free trade policies by the international financial institutions (Upchurch, 2008). The pursuit of flexibility has become a catechism for employers, with a 'normal' model of full-time employed workers employed by one company probably now looking abnormal from a global perspective. Employees' grip on their jobs has been loosened: even in Japan and South Korea, for many workers, lifetime employment has been eroded and replaced by precarious work forms. The widespread creation of 'informal' work has created a large pool of almost exclusively non-union workers. This in turn threatens unions' legitimacy in their wider function as representatives of the wide interests of labour rather than of particular groups of employees.

The veteran trade unionist Hans Gottfurcht, a leader with enormous experience of international union affairs wrote on our subject in the mid-1960s, and his accounts exuded optimism (Gottfurcht, 1962; 1966). Trade unions, he proclaimed, 'stand in the centre of world events' (1966: 12). There were objective grounds for his up-beat statement: trade unionism stood at an historically high level, and between the publication of his books in 1962 and 1966 an internationally coordinated strike involving the chemical workers' international occurred. It is hard to see similar grounds for optimism today. Multinational companies' growing power and the reduction in labour's share of global product both point in a more pessimistic direction. Despite much discussion of 'union renewal', the historic institutions of the labour market – trade unions and employers' associations – have been in retreat in most countries for several decades. These developments affect unions' capacity to act in workers' interests at all levels, including the international. J.K. Galbraith (1983) noted that historically, great concentrations of power such as that collectively wielded by large corporations today tend to produce countervailing forces. Whether the union internationals can constitute such a force, or even be one element in a wider coalition, is an open question that is explored below.

The broad family of international trade union institutions consists of the Global Union Federations (GUFs) and the International Trade Union Confederation (ITUC).

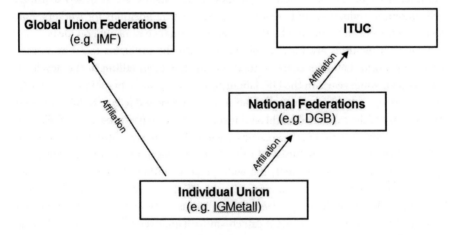

Diagram 1: National and International Levels of Trade Unionism

GUFs are distinguished by industrial sector, with national unions from over one hundred and twenty countries affiliating to them. Harold Lewis, ex-general secretary of the international transport workers has argued that GUFs account for 80 per cent of the international movement's activity, and at least 90 per cent of its work directly affecting workplaces (Lewis, 2003). The sectors covered range from education where Education International represents teachers, to transport, where the International Transport Workers' Federation is active. The GUFs are diverse organisations which share many characteristics. They can be grouped into three categories. The first is those with a private sector membership and an industrial and bargaining focus (BWI, ICEM, IMF, IUF and UNI). The second category (IFJ and ITGLWF) also have private sector members, but have less bargaining focus because they have a weak and unstable membership base. The third (EI and PSI) encompasses public sector unions, which relate mainly to international governmental organisations and national governments and have solid membership bases. In this book, the focus is on the first two categories because they operate primarily in the private sector.

Table 1: List of Global Unions, 2008

Global Union	Main Sectors Covered	Estimated Total Membership (Millions)	Total Number of Affiliates	Number of Countries Covered	Estimated Number of Developing Country Affiliates	Estimated Percentage of Developing Country Affiliates
ITUC	Umbrella body	168	311	155	190	61
EI	Education	30	394	171	189	48
IMF	Metalworking	25	200	100	Unknown	Unknown
ICEM	Chemicals, energy, mining, paper	20	379	117	182	48
PSI	Public services	20	650	160	323	50
UNI	Telecoms, graphics, media, retail, services	15.5	900	140	Unknown	Unknown
BWI	Construction and materials	12	318	130	Unknown	Unknown
ITGLWF	Textiles, garments, leather goods	9	238	122	163	68
ITF	Transport	4.5	654	148	63	10
IUF	Food, agriculture, catering, tourism	2.6	375	127	206	55
IFJ	Journalism	0.6	117	100	43	37

Source: Union websites

The book also touches on the work of the ITUC, created by merger in 2006, which works with the GUFs. The ITUC affiliates national centres, is relatively well resourced and is the largest umbrella organisation in the world. These are the established global organisations representing labour's interests, which are collectively referred to as 'the internationals'. When we refer to GUFs alone, we mean to exclude the ITUC.

GUF functions can be split into three types. First, they defend the existing space in which unions operate, for example by defending trade unionists' basic rights in extremely hostile environments. Second, they work to create further space, for example by collective bargaining (Wills, 2002). This set of tasks currently looms large in their own perceptions of their role even though GUFs have influence rather than power in relation to companies. Third, they help unions to exploit these spaces, primarily by building their capacities through educational and information activities. These functions are shown in Diagram 2.

Functions	Methods
Create space for local unions	IFAs
Defend space for local unions	Solidarity work
Demonstrate to unions how to move into space	Education

Diagram 2: GUF Functions

The internationals are coordinating bodies that link, or articulate, unions at other levels to each other and to international institutions and employers (Eder, 2002). Although the GUFs are formally described as 'global', this represents an aspiration rather than a reality since they are more accurately described as international bodies with wide coverage that are 'globalising'. They have historically built outwards from their European bases to include unions in other regions and are still engaged in extending their coverage to every country where unions exist. The GUFs both co-exist with and transcend the bilateral links that often spring up between individual unions across the world. Central to our argument is the view that only the multilateral frameworks provided by these international union institutions can shift the balances of power that exist both between unions and between unions and employers. For some, less institutionalised international links between unions are often felt to be sufficient and even preferable. We argue against this view.

Despite over a century of activity many misunderstandings of the internationals' roles are evident. Most people engaged in workplace industrial relations have little knowledge or understanding of these organisations and many trade union members are not aware that their unions are affiliated to them. The internationals have partly themselves to blame: they are poor promoters of their own successes, operating quietly even when real gains are secured for affiliates. However, it is important to understand that, like other trade union bodies, they operate within harsh political environments, invariably experience a hostile press and are therefore reluctant to divulge information to the outside world. They emphasise internal democracy and accountability rather than external transparency. In the 2006 Global Transparency Initiative, the ITUC was ranked last of all the non-governmental organisations surveyed, with a 13 per cent transparency capacity. Data on their activities is therefore very difficult to come by. There is a need for greater information on these bodies, and this is an important aspect of what we set out to achieve in this book.

Existing writing, with a few honourable exceptions, can be broadly divided into two camps: advocates/advisers and critics. Those falling into the first have a firm grasp of the realities of life in the internationals, often derived from experience of working in them (see for example White, 2006). Their strength, an in-depth knowledge of an organisation, can also be a weakness, however, since they are often concerned uncritically to defend their institutions past or present. Thus, for example, Chip Levinson (1972), ex-general secretary of the then International Chemical and General Workers' Federation (ICEF), tended to overstate its international bargaining successes in the 1960s. In the second camp, some criticism is vehement, and is marked by questionable argumentation. For example John Logue (1980: 24) referred to 'parasitic elite junketing', which apparently involved 'taking your pretty secretary [or, for that matter, your plain wife] on expenses-paid trips'. This is integral to his view that such junketing is a key reason for the longevity of this level of unionism.

There is no shortage of writers with criticism and advice for trade unions but much of it at the international level is of little value because it is founded on weak empirical bases. In sharp contrast to unions at the national level, academics have only infrequently enjoyed long-term or close relationships with the international trade union movement. This is compounded by the lack of publicly available data about the work of the internationals due in part to the levels of secretiveness which they practice. In writing this book, for example, the authors often have to use ITUC data as comparable material is not available (or where available is too imprecise) for the GUFs – although we do so only when convinced that the two pictures are similar.

We agree that what Lewis (2003) calls 'the theoretical wasteland' of international trade unionism should be addressed. We make some contribution in this area, focussing on education and its role, but the wider development of theory is not our main purpose here. Rather, we try to present a realistic and empirically grounded picture of the internationals in order to raise the quality of debate about their future. We present new data on several aspects of the internationals' internal lives and external work in the global economy. These data come from numerous sources. First, they derive from over fifty formal and informal interviews with officials of the internationals and union activists from many countries of the world. Second, they have been drawn from a trawl of the internationals' official and semi-official working documents. Many of the latter are not routinely available to outsiders, but nor are they confidential and almost all of those referred to exist in the Library of the Friedrich Ebert Foundation in Bonn. These last data have been especially important to us. Third, we have used the archival resources of the Modern Records Centre at the University of Warwick, where the records of the International Transport Workers' Federation and other relevant organisations are deposited. Finally, we draw on our own extensive personal records based on immersion in international union work over a period of fifteen years, some directly for the internationals and some less directly. We count many of those active in the international trade union movement as friends, and part of what we analyse is our own activity.

The book is structured and argued as follows. The next two chapters constitute the first section and provide background to the current situation. In Chapter two, the context in which unions and the internationals operate is outlined, showing why national unions are increasingly turning to the GUFs for assistance and illustrating the considerable extent of the demands on them. In Chapter three, we explore the internationals' history, showing the distinctive legacy they draw on to sustain them, and the significant new opportunities created by the end of political divisions symbolised by the recent creation of the ITUC.

Our second section is concerned with the current position of the internationals both internally and in relation to companies. In Chapter four, we analyse the internationals' resources and governance, explaining the twin problems of an internal balance of forces weighted towards developed country unions and major current financial issues. Chapter five examines their role in international collective bargaining. We show that the International Framework Agreements that currently play such a large role in their strategy are useful, but are generated by processes that reflect the power relationships described in the previous chapter and hamper their effectiveness. In Chapter six, we examine the company and regional industrial networks established through the GUFs and we suggest how they may best be built.

Chapter seven is concerned with education and is central to the book's argument. We propose that education is an important, polyvalent area of work that supports all of the other activities outlined previously. Importantly, it has a democratising effect by raising levels of participation in union affairs and could usefully be expanded. We therefore reject the common suggestion within the internationals that the GUFs' main task should be international collective bargaining. Chapter eight is intended both to illustrate and integrate our argument. It is also a contribution to wider discussions of the dynamics of international business. An extended case study, it shows how one GUF succeeded in building dialogue with a major multinational company, combining GUF discussion with senior management with organisation from below, strongly facilitated by educational work in Africa and Latin America.

Our third section consists simply of the conclusion. We accept that developments in the global political economy offer prospects for the internationals in building more multifaceted forms of unionism (Fairbrother and Hammer, 2005). We argue that this is best done using the educational approach we advocate which should be developed, and partly funded by devolving fundraising to regions. This educational work can most effectively be carried out by small groups of countries operating together on a 'minilateral' basis within the internationals' wider multilateral framework.

Our conclusion is presented as a challenge to the internationals' membership: to raise their material contribution to the internationals, despite the current trend in the opposite direction. The key players are the unions of the developed world, and the issue is whether they are able to make the political case to their own membership to intensify their commitment to internationalism.

CHAPTER TWO

Globalisation and Unions

Introduction

THIS chapter highlights the difficult international environment in which unions currently operate, without attempting a comprehensive analysis of global capitalism and its effects on workers and unions such as that by Moody (1997). It is divided into two sections. In the first, we sketch the consequences of globalisation's political dimension for workers and unions, stressing the weakening of national employment regulation and the lack of any adequate compensatory measures at global level. In the second, we examine both the problems and possibilities created for unions by multinational companies' practices. We conclude that it is difficult for unions to solve their problems either at national level or through bilateral links with other individual unions, causing them to increase the demands they make on the internationals.

Globalisation

The definition and consequences of globalisation are contested (Gills, 2000). The processes, it has been shown, require precise specification in more than one sense. Rugman (2001) for example contends that the companies involved should be conceptualised as 'regional', since many operate across only a few, often adjacent, countries. Others suggest that the current wave of globalisation constitutes less of a break with the past than is often supposed, since the internationalisation of trade and multinational companies are long-term phenomena. The history of capitalism has been characterised over three centuries by constant expansion in a geographical sense and in terms of its extension to ever-wider areas of social relations (Sewell, 2008). Capitalism has long sought 'spatial fixes' to labour problems: where workers become organised in one location, new locations are identified (Silver, 2003).

Between 1850 and 1914, the movement of capital, trade, immigration and flow of information were all arguably more developed than today (Hirst and Thompson, 2002), and this suggests a need to define the current wave's specific features. One key difference is that developing countries' systems of protection from competition are today weaker than under colonialism. As late as the immediate post-Second World War years, strong American pressure to end the British system of imperial protection, in favour of the current General Agreement on Tariffs and Trade (GATT), was effectively resisted (Toye, 2003). The current globalisation wave is characterised by the international financial institutions' discouragement of protectionist behaviours by developing countries. Indeed, the financial aspects of globalisation have profound consequences not only for national regulation, but also for companies and how they access and manage labour. Opening economies to international trade has had demonstrably negative effects on trade unions (Mosley and Uno, 2007).

If some have played down the globalisation phenomenon and sought carefully to delimit its boundaries, another school of thought has emphasised the current political influence and pervasiveness of neoliberal ideas. Thus, it has been argued that the globalisation process should be understood more widely than simply the unimpeded flow of capital and goods between countries, since it includes a wide range of other phenomena and, in particular, a major political dimension (Carling, 2006). Globalisation is seen as rooted in liberal economic theory, whereby the increasing liberalisation of trade is held to enhance wealth and to 'develop' those parts of the world to which it extends. The perspective is especially relevant to unionisation, whose fortunes have historically been strongly affected by the political environment (Western, 1997).

In this accommodating climate, 'free market' organisations have moved on to moral high ground previously occupied by others. Organisations like the Bill and Melinda Gates Foundation deploy considerable resources to present themselves as having an increasingly 'developmental' role in the world economy (Blowfield and Frynas, 2005), an agenda previously claimed by nationalism, social democracy and their historic allies. They propose a progressive, visionary, reforming agenda. 'Development' is seen by them not as the task of a developmental state in alliance with unions, but of these charitable foundations, markets, multinationals and increased trade.

From the late 1970s onwards, corporations sought new production locations where costs could be reduced and products marketed, and the international financial institutions created space for them by insisting on bi- and multilateral trade agreements. They pressured developing countries to reduce tariff barriers and allow unrestricted flows of capital, products and services. Structural Adjustment Programmes, repackaged as Poverty Reduction Strategy Papers, offered loan finance from the 1980s onwards, on condition of major reform and, in particular, a reduced role for the state. The ex-colonial powers are also implicated, as Stone (2004) showed, by pushing African states towards the IMF when they insist on enforcing harsh performance criteria as the condition of loans.

Many states shifted towards 'free market' politics, and the effects on both employment and unionisation have been considerable. In Africa, for example, they included the destruction of large parts of national healthcare and education systems, weakening workers in the employment relationship by making them more dependent on the health insurance and treatment that potentially came with formal employment. Much of manufacturing industry was destroyed, reducing the scope of and possibilities for unionisation. Unemployment rose dramatically in many countries as public sector workers were dismissed. Currency devaluations reduced real wages. Labour law was often revised in ways that were negative for trade unionism, while formal laws protecting employees were unenforceable by emasculated states (Wood and Brewster, 2007). Similar effects have occurred more widely. In many countries, minimum wages have fallen into disrepute, so weakly enforced have they become (Grindling and Terrell, 2005). Other pro-labour legislation has simply gone unobserved. The South Korean Equal Employment Act 1987, for example, obliges employers to provide facilities for childcare at workplaces, yet workplace childcare constitutes only one per cent of the total number of these facilities (Moon, 2006). In such cases, governments are clearly more concerned with employers' reactions to legal enforcement than with the legitimacy of their own law-making.

Symbolic of the current relationship between governments in the developing world and multinationals has been the development of Export Processing Zones (EPZs). These are areas where foreign companies are encouraged through incentives to operate and labour laws are either suspended or not enforced. They have grown considerably: by 2002 there were 3,000 EPZs employing more than 40 million workers, the great majority of whom were young women (Abott, 1997; ICFTU, 2003). Attempts to organise unions in EPZs have been met by violence from local security guards and police (ICFTU, 2003). Lim (2005) argues that multinationals have not been 'innocent bystanders' in determining the conditions that governments impose within EPZs.

The freedom of association and the right to collective bargaining, both Core Labour Standards in the International Labour Organisation's estimation, are under growing threat at a global level. Many countries, including the USA, India and China have refused to ratify the ILO conventions (87 and 98) that specify these basic rights. We show the countries who have signed the conventions in Map 1. Even among the surprisingly small number of signatory countries, there are several in which there have been high levels of complaints that they have not been observed. The results for unions are obvious. For the GUFs, this means an increasing volume and difficulty of solidarity work, where companies and governments are the object of protest on behalf of trade unions and their members alleging breach of these rights.

Recent legal changes in many countries have allowed employers to create fuzzy employment relationships and diffuse and precarious forms of work. These forms of employment are strongly associated with the growth of informal work that is a further distinctive feature of the current wave of globalisation. 'Informality' here means disguised, ambiguous or poorly defined employment relationships where employers are unclear or entirely absent (Chen, 2007). The phenomenon is very widespread: in Asia,

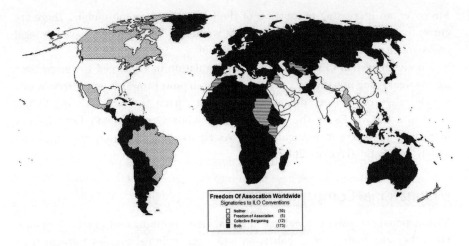

Map 1: Freedom of Association in the World

Latin America and Sub-Saharan Africa, informal workers now constitute between 60 and 70 per cent of the total working population. Few of these workers operate in total isolation from companies; their conditions are generally determined by the lead firm in the value chain, either a large national or multinational company (Chen, 2007). A pool of workers has therefore been created who find contract, agency or self-employed terms relatively attractive. As Lourenço-Lindell (2002) graphically illustrates in her detailed account of informal workers' lives in Guinea-Bissau, many of whom also work in the formal part of the economy when possible, they are 'walking a tightrope' where falling off means being unable to sustain their livelihoods.

Although unions have made efforts to recruit those working informally, these attempts have brought only very limited success (Verma and Kochan, 2004). The barriers are formidable: fierce competition between individuals, the heterogeneity of the workers involved and hard-line patriarchal attitudes are just a few of the problems (Wood and Frynas, 2006). Anyemedu (2000) identified a central issue of concern to unions in trying to organise these workers, that of high organising costs in relation to any possible subscription income. The workers fear harsh retaliation from employers and state officials if they join unions, threatening their very existence. Even if they do join, they are unable to pay realistic union subscriptions.

The current wave of globalisation is also characterised by a dramatic increase in the world labour supply. Vast amounts of extremely cheap labour, notably in the former Soviet Union, China and India, are now available to companies. There has been a tripling of the labour available to multinationals from around one billion people in 1980 to some three billion post-2000. This resulted not only from the collapse of Communism, but also from the opening up of economies to world capital and greater participation of women in waged labour (Munck, 2004).

Moreover, an increasing proportion of the labour has become mobile. There are currently an estimated 86 million migrant workers, who commonly have few legal employment rights (Lowell, 2007; UNDP, 2008).

No global system of protective worker regulation has emerged to compensate for the weakening of national systems and shift in power towards employers. While a wide range of advisory documentation exists, from the long-standing OECD guidelines for MNCs to the International Labour Organisation's Core Labour Standards, these are merely guidelines. As Hyman suggests, they are 'weak and largely tokenistic' (Hyman, 2002: 1).

Multinational Companies

Multinational companies loom large in global union thinking for five sets of reasons. First, they are engines of globalisation with high political profiles through their role in linking investment, trade, technology and finance. Second, they are often unionised in part of their operation and a foothold therefore exists that can be deepened. Third, there is a demand from companies for GUFs' work. The companies themselves are aware of a need both to coordinate their human resource policies worldwide and of the risks that labour issues pose for them. Extended value chains with links into the informal economy increase their exposure to this 'labour risk'. Fourth, as our case study in Chapter eight illustrates, senior trade unionists and MNC managers often have mutual long-term professional acquaintance. This may come from previous industrial relations dealings, or from discussion on a relatively equal and informal footing at the Davos World Economic Forum. These contacts have frequently established mutual knowledge of their organisations as well as personal lines of communication. In short, they are far more accessible to GUFs than the informal economy, helping to explain why a high proportion of GUF resources are spent in targeting them. Fifth, dialogue with central management in international companies is a significant, identifiable service that GUFs can offer affiliates.

However, just one per cent of the world's workforce of three billion people is employed by multinational companies (Köhler, 2003). At present, multinationals remain a strictly limited phenomenon in geographic and employment if not in trade terms. They largely carry out their business in the Triad of North America, Europe and Japan (Rugman, 2001). In 2005, all but four of the top 50 multinationals were headquartered in the Triad, although multinationals have begun to emerge from countries outside of it (UNCTAD, 2008). Many MNCs only expand to nearby countries; for example, one of the world's largest multinationals, the anti-union Wal-Mart, has most of its foreign investments in Canada. Multinational investment in the developing world is concentrated in Asia and Latin America (UNCTAD, 2008). MNC incidence is also to some extent sectoral. The Russian food sector is dominated by them, as are extractive industries in Africa, but their presence remains smaller in developing countries' railways. Multinationals are however growing: 73 million people worked for them in 2006 compared with 25 million in 1990. The World Bank projected that MNCs will increase considerably in extent and importance over the next twenty-five years (World Bank, 2007). For unions, work in them may represent as much an investment for the future as for the present.

As we noted above, the internationalisation of companies and trade has been a long-run process spanning several centuries. The trading companies of the eighteenth and early nineteenth century gave way to multinationals in manufacturing, utilities, services and extractive industries that expanded greatly in the inter-war years (Wilkins, 1974). The largest and most rapidly expanding activity in the 1950s and 1960s was in the colonial world's extractive industries (Jones, 1993). However, as Wilkins (1974) shows, these companies were rarely sufficiently powerful to challenge governments. In fact, governments actively sought on occasions to restrict strongly their operations and even expropriate them. In 1938, the Mexican oil industry, previously the preserve of multinationals was nationalised, providing a niche for Mexican unions, in a successful operation that provided a model for other countries. Costa Rica operated a system of state monopoly over the importation and marketing of petrol throughout the 1920s and 1930s (Odell, 1968). From the mid-1950s to the early 1970s many countries such as Egypt, Algeria and Burma, expanded their state sectors as nationalisations were carried out in areas considered vital to their national economies. Current 'resource nationalism' is a real force but generally stops short of nationalisation.

In a growth wave from the 1970s onwards, MNCs greatly increased their economic activity; by the early 1990s their accumulated sales were equivalent to one-third of the world's gross product (Buckley, 2000). These corporations ushered in the current era, since they were operating in a diversified set of industries, with an increasingly strong emphasis on services (Rugman, 2001; UNCTAD, 2008). Their influence on governments now came to be seen in stronger terms than previously; the end of the Cold War meant that there was no alternative to attempting to attract their investment. Their control of advanced technology means that their presence is now seen as a requirement for development; as a result, multinationals have become 'rule givers' in relation to governments (Thelen, 2006).

Multinationals, and especially US-based companies, argue publicly and privately for the relaxation of employment law. The changes in labour law recently enacted by the Chinese government, the Employment Contract Law 2007 and the Labour Disputes Arbitration Law 2007, which included some clauses providing the state unions with the opportunity to acquire some representative functions brought vigorous protest from the American Chamber of Commerce and threats that companies would disinvest. The equivalent organisation in Germany similarly presses for relaxations in labour law (Singe and Croucher, 2004). However, as the Chinese example shows, nation states continue to legislate in employment areas in ways not approved by international business. The nation state is therefore not always anxious simply to attract foreign investment at any price and outcomes are negotiated even if the balance in the negotiation has swung towards foreign companies.

Multinationals are popular employers in host countries. The differential paid by MNCs over local companies, after controlling for the industry involved, is large, and largest where average wages in the host countries are lowest. In the lowest income countries, employees in US-based multinationals earn twice as much as those in domestic companies (Graham, 2000). Differentials are especially marked in relatively hi-tech or high value-added sectors (Flanagan, 2006). Shell and BP, widely criticised for their activities in Nigeria, are nevertheless pay leaders in that country (Otobo, 2007). These advantages are often multiplied by access to company-based or assisted education and healthcare.

MNCs use much more labour than they employ, as capital markets impose performance regimes that demand cost reductions and push them towards accessing pools of cheap, 'informal' labour (Morgan and Kristensen, 2006). In addition, new forms of finance seek rates of return higher than those traditionally expected by investors (as they are often legally obliged to do), and simultaneously to escape even stock market regulation. An important form of such finance is 'private equity', and it has been estimated that some 20 per cent of the UK's non-public workforce is employed by these vehicles (Rossman and Greenfield, 2006). Private equity's influence clearly raises investors' expectations of appropriate rates of return and erodes commitment to other stakeholders. It has been shown that private equity has raised rates of redundancy across the world (Hall, 2008).

Theron (2005) uses the term 'externalisation' to encompass the different ways of obtaining labour from outside of the corporation's boundaries. Its extent at global level has unfortunately not been the subject of any systematic investigation (Mosley and Uno, 2007). Labour outsourcing is increasingly being required of local management by multinationals' central managements (Westney, 2008). Externalisation virtually removes the direct claims that workers can make of them. Externalised workers are rarely protected by law in the same ways as 'standard' workers, because in almost all countries the law envisages a 'standard' employment relationship. Externalisation takes many forms, many of which are in reality not discrete, and its incidence and damaging consequences for workers and unions alike have been widely remarked on by researchers examining the developing world (Wood and Brewster, 2007; von Holdt and Webster, 2005; Theron, 2005). The creation of 'value chains' from the MNC at the top down to tiny family concerns, sub-contractors or individual 'own account' workers inexorably drives the overall share of labour in company earnings downwards (Barrientos, 2002). The ends of these chains contain a good deal of 'labour risk' for companies. An American researcher linked cars sold in Canada back through car manufacturing multinationals to the Brazilian steel industry and slavery in the Brazilian charcoal industry (Bales, 2004).

Thus, the multinationals are linked, both directly and indirectly, to the 'informal' economy. Intermediaries have oiled the wheels of this process. In many countries legislation was enacted in the 1980s that facilitated the activities of labour agencies (Glyn, 2006). Thus, even in highly regulated Germany, the number of agency workers has risen from just over 100,000 in 1993 to 630,000 in 2007 (Bundesinstitut für Arbeit, 1993; 2007). Seventy per cent of the workers used by Nestlé to manufacture, package and distribute products throughout the world are not directly employed by that company (Rossman and Greenfield, 2006). As we noted above, reliable global figures on the extent of externalised labour do not exist (ILO, 2007) but their growth may be simply illustrated by the extent of the multinational companies that supply it, shown in Table 2 below:

Table 2: Key Multinationals Supplying Labour

Multinational	2004	2006/7
Adecco	5,800 offices	7,000 offices 2007
Manpower	4,300 offices	4,400 offices 2007
Vedior *	2,200 offices	2,433 offices 2006
Randstad		1,827 offices 2006 2,670 offices 2007

Note: * Vedior was purchased by Randstad in December 2007
Source: ICEM (2004); company annual reports and websites

The labour-supplying multinationals whose empires are indicated in Table 2 are clearly only the formal, visible part of labour contracting; a wide range of labour suppliers in the developing world constitute the submerged part of that iceberg. These intermediaries form part of a nexus of corruption in obtaining contracts, criminality and violence in Colombia (Pearce, 2004). Lourenço-Lindell (2002) describes the extensive activities of agents called 'headmen' in Guinea-Bissau, who first negotiate for work from employers in competition with other headmen, and then select labour and supervise tasks.

These work forms condition workers' and managers' expectations of acceptable standards of terms, conditions and treatment. In direct employment terms, MNCs can thus remain 'model' employers, and 'employers of choice', while distancing themselves from their suppliers and indeed the suppliers of suppliers where conditions are very different. The minority of employees in the company's direct employment are well aware of their privileged status. MNCs are able to raise productivity partly because they tie employees into their ways of working. Thus, many MNCs follow a dual policy: ending or avoiding the employment relationship for the majority of employees, and improving pay to well above local levels for the minority they choose directly to employ. This is a new aspect of the current wave of globalisation.

There are however limits to the process. The extent to which it can be required depends on the extent to which the company's success is perceived as reliant on developing the long-term commitment of its labour force. It is only minimally practised in some high value-added companies such as the German-owned motor manufacturers. These operate with a more cooperative labour paradigm which facilitates union involvement and employee representation at all levels.

Multinationals' direct policies in relation to unions reflect at least to some extent their countries of origin. US-based companies favour countries where wages are lower, where it is easiest to shed labour and the industrial relations environment is seen as benign (Cooke, 1997; Bognanno et al., 2005). The last characteristic is measured in terms of the extent of local union influence, though MNCs are more favourably disposed to company-based forms of representation such as works councils. As we show in Chapter five, European-based multinationals are relatively friendly towards unions. This is related to the form of human resource management (HRM) that they adopt and the extent to which they attempt to dictate the form from the company's headquarters. There are essentially two forms of HRM. One is 'collaborative'. This has a developmental or humanistic focus, where employees are seen as partners or collaborators. On the other hand, there is 'calculative' HRM in which employees are treated as a resource. Calculative HRM centres on the accurate measurement of employee contributions to the firm, and the adoption of individually based reward systems (Gooderham et al., 1999). It sidelines unions since individual pay is not conducive to traditional forms of collective bargaining.

In Europe, foreign companies (which are mostly US-based) more commonly follow 'calculative' HRM than domestic companies (Gooderham et al., 1999; 2006). US-based companies in less-skilled sectors tend to follow centralised union exclusion policies. Thus, McDonald's has successfully resisted unionisation in many national contexts (Royle, 2005; 2006). In the failed attempt to unionise the McDonald's greenfield food processing factory in Moscow, the few activists involved received significant material, publicity and moral support from the global union, the IUF (Royle, 2005). McDonald's may constitute an exceptional company, but similar policies have been applied by other US-based companies with relatively low-skilled workforces such as Wal-Mart, even in highly regulated Germany (Köhnen and Glaubitz, 2000). In Ireland, they follow similar policies largely through setting up on greenfield sites (Turner et al., 2002).

Anti-union policies pushed by central managements may occasionally be resisted at local level. A recent work suggests that local managers can defend and advance subsidiaries' influence in alliance with unions. Kristensen and Zeitlin (2005), in their study of APV, a manufacturing multinational based in the UK with subsidiaries in the USA and Denmark, argue that the Danish subsidiary achieved a strategic role in the company by using their links to many different local actors. The union was a key ally for local management, helping improve the company's access to skilled labour locally and actively helping management strategise. The prescription these authors offer, of a MNC involved in facilitating dialogue between itself and employees through representative institutions is, they admit, an unlikely prospect. The setting was exceptionally favourable for such an alliance. The Danish model provides considerable possibilities for union representatives not only through the 1973 law providing for employee representatives' election to company boards, and through European Works Councils, but also by well-established, historically deeply rooted norms.

Outside such exceptional environments, and especially outside of the developed world, local management pursues *less* union-friendly models than central management. Even when written into collective agreements, local managers adopt 'flexible' interpretations of relatively clear rights such as those to freedom of association and collective bargaining. The latter may be formally espoused at headquarters level, and then, to adopt the terms used by a team of management scholars, 'ceremonially' adopted or 'lost in translation' locally (Fenton O'Creevy et al., 2007). Thus, for example, managers in countries such as Russia and Mexico, where company-based unions are widespread, interpret allowing company unions as complying with central values favouring the freedom of association. They thereby marginalise or exclude forms of unionism centred on mobilising workers and meaningful bargaining. In Russia, this entails, at worst, union forms designed to discipline workers and, at best, welfare-oriented unions. In this scenario, collective bargaining consists of essentially administrative discussions about a 'collective agreement' that specifies little and cannot be enforced.

Multinationals pose problems for unions at national level because of many of these companies' capacity to threaten to shift location, to play one unit off against another and to distribute investment according to local performance. These possibilities are clearly more available in some sectors than others but many MNCs, as we saw above, are currently located in services rather than in the location-bound extractive sector and can therefore threaten this with credibility. Martinez-Lucio and Weston (2004) have argued that even in the highly regulated European context, the dynamics set up by this possibility are often very difficult for unions to overcome.

In general however, and despite these problems, MNCs are relatively well unionised in the developing world when compared to domestic companies. The most systematic study of the subject demonstrates that they more readily recognise unions, and direct investment by them brings better labour relations (Mosley and Uno, 2007). Their importance also underlines the internationals' significance to national unions; the latter draw on the GUFs' expertise in dealing with them. The expansion of multinationals' international reach serves to remind many trade unionists, particularly in the developing world, of how intimately the fates of their national unions and the internationals are intertwined.

Conclusion

The consequences for unions of the current wave of globalisation have been severe. Many of the old certainties and structural supports for trade unionism have been removed. The predominance of neoliberal economic ideas has reduced union political influence. MNCs have become more assertive in relation to national governments than in previous waves of globalisation, while the growth of informal work has diminished union membership and economic power.

The possibilities of unions dealing with their problems at national level have clearly decreased. National regulation has far less mileage than hitherto and unions have therefore turned to the international level for solutions (O'Brien, 2000).

Developing country unions have also continued to develop bilateral links with other unions, often from the ex-colonial countries. But these links are much less likely to offer viable solutions since the internationals have greater capacity to generate comprehensive information about multinationals. Nor do they occur within the internationals' democratic framework. Still less can links with a few developed country unions offer prospects of organising among informal workers, where these unions have little or no experience. These resilient problems are better addressed by the internationals, with their breadth of experience and expertise in the developing world. Whether they have the resources or governance mechanisms to address them in optimal ways is a question we discuss in Chapter four.

CHAPTER THREE

Past and Present – the History of International Trade Unionism

Introduction

THIS chapter deals with the history of the international trade union movement's institutions, to locate our contemporary analysis in that context. The history of all these bodies is part of their organisational culture, as their headquarters' walls covered with posters of twentieth-century campaigns demonstrate. Despite some useful contributions, no adequate overall history of this level of trade unionism exists. With a few honourable exceptions (exemplified by the work of Tony Carew (1987; 2000; 2007) Rebecca Gumbrell-McCormick (2000a; 2000b; 2001; 2004) and Marcel van der Linden (2000)), previous accounts have occurred in separate 'historical' and 'current' silos. Yet certain enduring themes are apparent, implying profound structural issues. On the other hand, the current situation has novel characteristics, not least because of the relative political unity of the world's unions after the collapse of Communism in 1989.

Our arguments in this chapter are as follows: first, history shows a significant sequence in the formation of different bodies, reflecting their relative weight in the thinking of national unions. Second, we argue that it is not the case, as some have suggested, that the structures devised between the late 1890s and 1903 'remained largely unchanged' in the twentieth century (van der Linden, 2000: 528). This refers simply to the dual structure with an international umbrella organisation and industry-based bodies. It ignores the existence of rival international structures for much of the twentieth century, which rendered cooperation across the political divide next to impossible. The inception of the division constituted a *dis*continuity of major importance. This political division in the international union movement that appeared soon after the Russian Revolution has now disappeared, creating new opportunities. Third, the internationals have long, rich histories which have stamped their individual and collective identities and, importantly, underpin a long-term view by unions of payoffs from membership. Long organisational histories encourage affiliates to see the benefits of affiliation in the long-term rather than to look for short-term benefits. Finally, we suggest that a certain version of the history, emphasising the internationals' collective role in the fights against Fascism and Apartheid functions as a sustaining resource.

Origins

The first wave of institutional international union cooperation occurred in the third quarter of the nineteenth century, at the beginnings of an earlier intense phase of globalisation. National markets had not yet been finally consolidated in Europe and America and major imperial projects such as the 'scramble for Africa' had yet to begin.

Marx's international, the International Working Men's Association (IWMA), formed in 1864, therefore operated in a context in which the need for such a body was less self-evident than it was later to become. Marxist language and ideals live on as a set of shared reference points in international trade union discourse, including in its symbols such as the singing of the *Internationale* at some international union gatherings. The IWMA and its successors provided intellectually powerful alternatives to the nationalistic, racially based and imperialist ideas being pursued not only by employers and ruling élites, but then accepted in wide sections of the trade union movement. These ideas found expression in many damaging ways, including in racially based unions in many parts of the world (Kirk, 2003).

Marx's project attracted some affiliation and support from sections of the European trade union movement, faced by employers importing cheaper foreign labour from neighbouring countries. The IWMA also established relations (albeit fractious) between political internationalists and trade unions, which paved the way for the Second Social Democratic International. Trade union internationalism, although not initiated by Marxists, therefore found its first institutional form under Marxist leadership although, as Marx well knew, the policies of the IWMA were too advanced and idealistic for the pragmatic British union leaders. This highlighted what was to be a long-standing tension between the industrial interests and national orientations of most union leaders on the one hand, and those of the more political internationalists on the other (Collins and Abramsky, 1965). It already implied the enduring question of precisely how strong or autonomous an international could be: how much power would be ceded by national unions, fearful of having policy determined by those holding an alternative conception? The issue's significance was underlined by the interest of rival political streams in international trade unionism such as the anarchists and Christians.

Diagram 3: Timeline – the History of the International Trade Union Movement

International union movement	World events
1864: International Working Men's Association formed	
1871: Delegates of Austrian, German and Scandinavian shoemakers sign cooperation agreement	1871: German victory in Franco-Prussian War; Unification of Germany
1876: International Working Men's Association dissolved	
	1881: Second International founded
1889: International Trade Secretariats of shoemakers, printers, hatters, tobacco workers formed	
1897: International Transport Workers' federation formed	
1901: First conference of the International Secretariat of National Trade Union centres held	
1913: International Federation of Trade Unions founded	
1914: Over one hundred International Trade Secretariats in existence	
1914: 33 ITSs in existence	1914: Outbreak of First World War
1918–1920s: Many ITSs merge	1917: Russian Revolution
1919: IFTU re-constituted	1918: First World War ends
1919: International Federation of Trade Unions founded	
1920: International Federation of Christian Trade Unions (forerunner of WCL) formed	
1921: Red International of Labour Unions founded	
	1933: Nazis accede to power in Germany
1937: Red International of Labour Unions formally dissolved	1939: Outbreak of Second World War
1945: World Federation of Trade Unions formed	1945: Second World War ends
1949: International Confederation of Free Trade Unions formed	
1973: European TUC formed	
	1989: Soviet Union collapses
2006: WCL dissolved to merge with ICFTU and form the International Trade Union Confederation	

The Emergence of International Sectoral and Umbrella Bodies

The formation of the Second (Social Democratic) International created the political cohesion and contacts that precipitated the first international industrial organisations. In many continental European countries, trade unionism was a project launched by social democrats rather than, as in Britain, the reverse or, as in the USA, one that never generated a Labour Party (Robert, Prost and Wrigley, 2004). This is not to argue that the main concerns of the new international union organisations were political, since the contrary was the case as they were primarily interested in industrial matters. It is to suggest that the first viable institutions of internationalism were formed on a non-Marxist basis that nevertheless inherited some of Marxism's internationalist rhetoric.

As we show in the timeline, highly skilled craft trade unionists together with miners and textile workers were the first to initiate international organisations on an industrial basis from 1889 onwards. These were the GUFs' predecessors, the International Trade Secretariats (ITSs). The basis of the craft unions' organisation was strong occupational identities and capacity to restrict entry to their trades at local and national level. They felt a need for international coordination for pragmatic industrial as well as for political reasons. Huge vertically integrated cartels were emerging and expanding their international reach. Migrant labour was becoming increasingly important and threatened to undercut national unions' efforts, especially in continental Europe. In Germany, whose expanding economy was sucking in migrant workers from neighbouring countries, the issue was especially pressing and the majority of ITSs were based in Germany from their inception up until Hitler's accession to power in 1933.

However, the basis for international union organisation was rickety. At the end of the nineteenth century, national systems of trade unionism were still being consolidated: in Britain there were still movements for local autonomy in craft unions at the beginning of the twentieth century. In France, social democrats 'implanted' union organisation in rural areas (Robert, Prost and Wrigley, 2004). In short, strong elements of regionalism *within nations* remained in the unions seeking to establish international coordination (Dreyfus, 2000). The incomplete and uneven internal development of national systems until 1914 therefore formed a basis for ITSs founded on little more than information exchange and occasional mutual support of strike action.

The development of ITSs within industry sectors both preceded and precipitated the formation of an umbrella organisation for national union centres and reflects their importance to pragmatic unions in dealing with emergent international companies. The umbrella body began and continued as an organisation for more directly political purposes than the ITSs. This was the case even if the German and French unions that played a key role in establishing all of these bodies had very different conceptions of the purposes and methods of trade unionism. These unions built the next international umbrella venture, the International Secretariat of National Trade Union Centres (ISNTUC), to be renamed the International Federation of Trade Unions (IFTU) in 1913. The British stood aloof, but by 1913 the IFTU had grown to include twenty affiliated national centres, mostly in Europe but including the USA and the Transvaal (Fimmen, 1922).

The IFTU did not go far beyond exchanging information; the French conception of a more political and internationally solidaristic unionism was sidelined in favour of the more institutional and information-sharing form advocated by the Germans (Tudyka, 1983; Dreyfus, 2000). This remained influential in the IFTU even after the First World War, since it allowed national union centres to learn about each other and companies without being tied to any specific international policies.

By 1914, the current structure's broad outlines were visible: a set of industrial coordinating bodies, and an umbrella organisation bringing national centres together. So, too, were at least three of the significant abiding issues: unions' concern not to cede power; tensions between forms of trade unionism; and real political differences. The latter were soon to sharpen, generating a major and long-standing split in the international movement.

Division in the Movement: the RILU

The First World War had been preceded by dramatic strike waves in Europe that encouraged the development of revolutionary union ideas, or syndicalism. This in turn encouraged many to imagine that the strike weapon could be used for internationalist purposes. But the outbreak of war demonstrated the strictly rhetorical nature of the Social Democratic Second International's commitment to an international general strike in the event of war. The First World War brought massive political rupture. The Russian Revolution solidified the earlier breakaway of the Communists from the Social Democrats, a division that was to last, with only a brief interlude, for the next seventy years. This division was to be even more damaging than the one that had already emerged between the IFTU and the International Federation of Christian Trade Unions (IFCTU), whose relationship to the IFTU has been characterised as 'at times quite competitive and combative' (Tosstorff, 2005: 401). Thus, sharp political and religious rivalries were both present in the world's trade union movement from an early stage.

The social democratic and business forms of trade unionism took steps to advance and consolidate their position in response to a huge upturn in union membership during the First World War. Between April 1919 and August 1921, twenty-nine ITSs were established (van Goethem, 2000). The umbrella body also became much closer to a global coordinating body than hitherto. The fourteen countries represented at the founding congress of the IFTU in 1919 consisted essentially of the Europeans, plus the American Federation of Labour, self-appointed guardian of the Latin American movements that had joined the recently formed Pan American Federation of Labour (van Goethem, 2000; 2006). The Americans were determined to follow a resolutely industrial path, but the Europeans defeated them, insisting on the need for political action. But the IFTU, initially urged by the French CGT, was already taking this type of action in initiating discussions (from which they were subsequently excluded) that brought the establishment of the tripartite International Labour Organization (ILO).

The ILO was an important institution that was to provide a major forum for international labour issues. The IFTU, though disappointed at the watered-down form that the ILO assumed, soon set to its enduring task of lobbying it to create international labour standards (Tosstorff, 2005). The IFTU had thus helped create much of the water in which it and its descendants the ICFTU and ITUC were to swim. In 1921, the American Federation of Labour, dismayed at the political turn of events, notified the IFTU that it had decided not to affiliate (Fimmen, 1922). This marked the beginning of over two decades of widespread indifference among American unions towards the international trade union movement that was only to be overcome at the end of the Second World War. For the Communists, the same developments were interpreted in quite a different sense: the formation of the ILO was a sign that the mainstream unions had definitively sold out to the capitalist class.

In many countries, including Britain and the USA, the Communist parties absorbed many of the pre-war syndicalists, thereby acquiring some of the best and most active trade unionists. From the 1920s, the international Communist movement built its separate union institution, the Red International of Labour Unions (RILU). In 1921, the IFTU decided that any union affiliating to the RILU could not be admitted to the IFTU (Fimmen, 1922). A minority in the IFTU, led by its co-secretary and general secretary of the relatively well-developed International Transport Workers' Federation, Edo Fimmen, favoured opening a dialogue on the appropriate structure for the international movement. Fimmen's political outlook was on the cusp of social democracy and Communism and coloured by syndicalism (Buschak, 2002). To the consternation of many, he therefore advocated including the Soviet unions in the discussion.

Labour's Alternative

The issue was among those that brought Fimmen's resignation as IFTU co-secretary; it was only after resigning that he gained the freedom to write probably the most important document ever written on the international movement's structure, *Labour's Alternative* (1924). The majority of the work discusses developments in international capitalism, which 'imposed' and 'forced' change on unions. Earlier moves towards international cartels were now accelerating: 'Huge, octopus-like capitalist groups are extending their tentacles to grasp all the treasures of the world...' (p.10). Pre-1914, these only sought to dictate prices to consumers, but now they sought to dictate the price of labour. He defined the internationals' task as bargaining collectively with these groups, a prelude to collectivising the means of production through revolution.

For Fimmen, the IFTU–RILU division was central because it obstructed coordinated bargaining; post-1950, this argument was proven highly relevant. Other significant issues such as increasing the minimal involvement of women and colonial workers in trade unionism would be assisted by overcoming that key problem. Removing the division between the IFTU and RILU was, moreover, a condition for releasing the *resources* required to bring a more truly international organisation into being by persuading unions in the rest of the world to affiliate. Fimmen's emphasis on resources makes explicit an issue that remains relevant today. A new organisational basis was needed for this merged IFTU; the ITSs were a key ingredient because they mirrored capitalist organisation, but national union centres could not be ignored and he therefore advocated a combination of national centres and ITSs as a basis (pp.117–23). There is a notable and probably politic ambiguity here about the precise form that such an organisation would take, which allowed room for manoeuvre at a later stage.

Fimmen's ideas foundered on the very problem they addressed: the political split between Communists and Social Democrats. He had written the work at a time when it was still possible to argue as he did, because relations between the two sides had not degenerated too far. But from the defeat of the British General Strike in 1926 until the early 1930s, RILU encouraged breakaway unions and launched savage attacks on the 'reformist' and (more commonly) 'social fascist' or 'Amsterdam' unions. This poisoned relations and ruled RILU out of any constructive dialogue with either the IFTU or the majority of ITS affiliates. Fimmen, from his position in the transport workers, was left to continue to try to improve relations between the two warring sets of unions.

Free Trade Unionism and Communist Affiliations: from Divorce to Global Rivalry

From the mid-1920s, the unions throughout the international patchwork that was the Soviet Union were decisively stripped of their independence and subordinated to the Communist Parties. As Carew (1987) pointed out, Western unions were therefore right to regard them as not being free trade unions, even if Communist-led unions in the Western world could not be categorised in the same way. The Soviet unions became 'a school of Communism' and a 'transmission belt' of Communist policy. In the workplace, they became the welfare wing of management and exercised harsh discipline on dissidents. Internationally, these unions became instruments of Soviet foreign policy, as illustrated by the demise of the RILU itself. After the accession of Hitler to power in 1933 and the German unions' destruction, Stalin decided that a more conciliatory attitude towards the Social Democrats and the mainstream trade unions was required. RILU, which had started life as a genuinely independent body, was run down from 1934 onwards and quietly disbanded in 1937 because Stalin regarded it as an obstruction to his foreign policy (Tosstorff, 2004).

The Nazi's rapid demolition of the previously powerful German unions removed an important element in the international movement and sent tremors through the remainder. All of the ITSs, who had already been campaigning against Fascism since 1924, and who supported the Italian resistance, played a significant role in campaigning against Nazism. The ITF had demanded immediate action in defence of the German unions in 1933 by the IFTU but were defeated by the opposition of the German unions themselves (Simon, 1983; Reinalda, 1997). The ITF began publication of a multilingual publication, *Swastika* (soon to become *Fascism*), documenting the effects of Fascism on workers from 1934 to 1945. The transport workers' extensive worldwide networks were later used to good effect by the Allied governments in espionage during the Second World War (Koch-Baumgarten, 1997). The ITF was also the driving force in establishing a Joint Council of Propaganda between itself and the metalworkers' and miners' internationals to propagandise for free trade unionism in the occupied countries, an initiative that soon went beyond its original functions: by 1944, the Council was sending delegates to liberated France to influence the re-forming French unions.

The effects of Stalinism on workers were also understood in the international trade union élite. Meeting in the context of widespread pro-Soviet feeling in Britain after the invasion of the USSR, the Annual Meeting of the International Metalworkers' Federation in August 1942 attended by exiled trade unionists from numerous countries demonstrated their awareness. They heard and accepted without demur a speech by Sidney Parlett of the ILO, who argued that:

> The Russian representatives at an international gathering would only voice policy insofar as it found consent and endorsement from the Russian Communist Party. If, therefore, the workers were going to fight for a Charter of trade union rights for other countries, how could they rely on the unequivocal support of the Russian trade unions?

> (IMF, 1942)

The defeat of Nazism in 1945 brought a temporary and unstable unity in the international trade union movement, when for a brief period Social Democratic and Communist unions came together in the World Federation of Trade Unions (WFTU). But as the Cold War set in, the split between the Social Democratic and Communist streams re-established itself amid tumultuous and vituperative scenes (Hogan, 1989). One of the causes célèbres was the degree of independence to be given to ITSs; the Soviets argued for (and later adopted when they were left to themselves) a structure in which the ITSs would be integrated into the world body as 'trade departments'. This, of course, would have meant ceding considerable industrial influence to the Soviets, and was rejected; the ITSs were strongly opposed to having their autonomy reduced in this way (Windmuller, 1954; McShane, 1992).

The US government strongly encouraged the American unions to step up their activities in the international movement, and worked influentially against WFTU across a broad material and ideological front (Windmuller, 1954; Carew, 1987). However, as Denis McShane has argued, the European unions' own experiences had also been important in their rejection of Soviet influence (McShane, 1992). By 1950 WFTU was unquestionably dominated by the Soviet unions because major Western unions had left (Koftas, 2002). The International Confederation of Free Trade Unions (ICFTU) was formed on Anglo-American initiative and it and the WFTU went their separate ways, beginning an increasingly bitter war for the political affiliation of unions in the rest of the world. Both of them together with the third, relatively small but aggressive, International Federation of Christian Trade Unions (later World Confederation of Labour, WCL) now pursued their own rival agendas, competing for affiliations and trying to establish their own structures throughout the world.

WFTU was also influential in global terms. In the 1950s, it gave considerable material assistance to help found and maintain formally independent international associations, notably the International Confederation of Arab Trade Unions and the much stronger Congreso Permanente de Unidad Sindical de los Trabajadores de America Latina. In Africa, WFTU, after initial criticism of the Organisation of African Trade Union Unity, began to work closely with it (Lieβ, 1983). In India, the All-India Trade Union Congress was an affiliate. In Europe, the largest union confederations in France and Italy, the CGT and CGIL, were long-term full affiliates until the latter moved to associate membership. The CGIL gradually distanced itself from WFTU as part of a wider disillusionment on the part of Western trade unionists with the effects of their affiliation. The CGIL moved away because of declining strength and failure in its persistent efforts to secure unity in action in relation to employers with the other Italian union organisations who were strongly opposed to the CGIL's international affiliation (Rogari, 2000). After 1968, this sort of distancing became common among national unions.

The unions previously affiliated to IFTU formed a large part of the organisational basis for the creation of the International Confederation of Free Trade Unions (ICFTU) in 1949. The new title both reaffirmed unions' historic assertion of their independence from employers and the state and stressed the difference between themselves and unions in the Communist world. The ICFTU soon gained primacy within the international trade union movement in its role as the 'voice of labour', because of its use by governments as such in the restructuring of the post-War years (Gumbrell-McCormick, 2001). Other parts of the international movement now entered a period of steady increase in interest and affiliations. Thus, the Christian IFCTU expanded in the developing world, establishing a regional organisation in Latin America in the mid-1950s (Pasture, 1999). So, too did the ITSs, as we show for the ITF in Table 3.

Table 3: Number of ITF-affiliated Organisations by Region, 1946 and 1964

ITF region	1946	1964
Europe/Middle East	57	117
Latin America/Caribbean	5	99
Asia-Pacific	9	42
Africa	3	36
North America	3	18
Totals	77	312

Source: Lewis (2003: 360)

Regional organisations grouping countries together developed throughout the world, first in the ICFTU and later in the ITSs, to reflect the interests of the developing country membership within the international structures. Their creation increased the diversity of unions involved in the international movement. There was a feeling among some affiliates that the ICFTU as a global organisation was constantly trying to widen its functions beyond the coordinating role that they thought it suited to, but that its basis made it difficult for it to help unions locally. In 1966, the British TUC's international committee minuted:

> If the question of starting afresh arose the TUC – taking experience as a starting point – would perhaps not be in favour of establishing an organisation such as the ICFTU with its present functions, nor disposed to accept that the somewhat heterogeneous political attitudes of major ICFTU affiliates provide a satisfactory basis for common and large-scale operations directed towards developing countries.

(quoted in Carew, 2007: 163)

The judgement from the TUC's international committee may have underestimated the international movement's work. Through their structures in the world's regions, the ICFTU and ITSs built widespread educational activity to develop the skills and capacities of local unions to deal with their problems. The ICFTU had a long tradition of such work and soon began to use its Solidarity Fund, first set up in 1957, for educational purposes (Gottfurcht, 1966; Carew, 2000). A strong example of its activity was the coordinated efforts by the ICFTU and six GUFs to develop cadres in Indonesia in the late 1960s (Carew, 2000). Another example from this period was the substantial educational work of the ICFTU in Africa. The calibre of those carrying out this work was considerable; it was led by the Nigerian intellectual Wogu Ananaba, author of an impressive history of the African trade unions (CISL, 1972;

Ananaba, 1979). This educational work also importantly allowed the internationals to acquire detailed understandings of the world's very different unions.

In Europe, the heartland of the international movement, the growth of structures designed to coordinate European unions in part reflected an increasing feeling that the ICFTU was providing too little for the unions of the developed world, one of the underlying reasons for the Americans leaving it in the late 1960s (Carew, 2007). The development of the European Union stimulated a proliferation of bodies both outside and inside the existing organisations. The international movement was faced with the development of essentially parallel structures in the form of European Industry Federations and the European TUC. Thus, for example, between the late 1950s and 1983, nominally separate bodies for food, drink and tobacco workers existed both inside and outside of the IUF (Buschak, 2003). WFTU hoped that the development of these European-level bodies would improve relations with ICFTU affiliates, but these hopes proved groundless (Lieβ, 1983).

For the ICFTU, creation of the ETUC led to the loss of its existing European body (Gumbrell-McCormick, 2001). This created major tensions within the ICFTU as it struggled to decide how to deal with the new phenomenon. Ultimately, it decided not to take a position, which Gumbrell-McCormick (2000a) argues was a wise act of diplomacy and not simply inertia, since it allowed the ICFTU to maintain the world organisation's unity albeit at considerable cost. However, for some national trade union movements in Europe, the EU's increasing pull ushered in a period of greater orientation towards Europe to the exclusion of the rest of the world.

The international trade union movement was expanding beyond its hitherto narrow geographical base, as each side in the Cold War was trying to recruit unions. In Africa and Asia, unions often provided the mass base for nationalist movements to fight for independence from the European imperial powers, and the Americans and Soviets vied for their loyalty. The unions of Europe, the USA and the USSR pursued what was at least in part a Cold War political agenda in the rest of the world. Gary Busch (1983) argued that for the main governments involved, the importance of international trade unionism was second only to military intelligence. A consequence was that the ICFTU ruled out contact between itself and WFTU despite the wishes of some of its affiliates (Lieβ, 1983).

In some parts of the ex-colonial world such as Africa, the Cold War had serious consequences for trade unionism, weakening it wherever the US distributed economic or military aid (Koftas, 2002; Thomson and Larson, 1978). Wedin (1991), in a sensitive study of foreign union assistance in Latin America, shows how despite good intentions, foreign interventions at this time had negative effects and even 'victims'. Foreign subventions on occasions reduced union democracy to a farce (Croucher, 2003). In Kenya, for example, the nationalist politician and trade union leader Tom Mboya rapidly marginalised his political opponents with financial backing from the USA, finally removing them from the Kenya Federation of Trade Unions (Hagglund,

2007). In Japan, the Cold War also had important negative effects and the ICFTU affiliates became identified with the occupier. By 1950, the Communist union centre Sanbeyu was in the forefront of the Japanese trade union movement, but the American Military Government stimulated a breakaway centre, Sohyo. In the early 1950s, the American Military Government dismissed large numbers of public sector trade unionists in the name of removing Communist influence, but also included non-Communist unionists. This initiated a period lasting right up until the collapse of Communism, in which affiliation to the ICFTU or WFTU constituted a factional issue within Japanese unions described as 'damaging' (Carew, 2000: 218). Despite this sharp split, the ITSs were nevertheless able to provide a focus for coordinated action between Japanese enterprise-based unions. In 1964, the International Metalworkers' Federation established a Japan Council, playing a major part in establishing the annual 'spring offensive' (Park, 1983).

A combination of political and industrial rivalries weakened ITS attempts to confront the activities of multinationals. These attempts were the first signs that the international union movement was moving decisively towards attempting international collective bargaining despite the implied transfer of bargaining authority from national to international level. Charles 'Chip' Levinson, general secretary of the ICEF, seeking to raise the profile of his previously weak ITS (Gallin, 1997), confirmed this as the international movement's main task (Levinson, 1972). The North American United Auto Workers and the West German IG Metall pushed this agenda within the International Metalworkers' Federation while the ICEF and the IUF developed international campaigns directed at particular multinationals. World Company Councils were developed in some companies in the 1960s by the IMF and ICEF. Yet significant unions in France, Italy and India were excluded because they were affiliated to the WFTU (Leiβ, 1983). By 1988, a new approach emerged that allowed the preservation of national unions' bargaining independence and the first International Framework Agreement (IFA) was concluded by the IUF with BSN Danone in 1988 (Gumbrell-McCormick, 2000a; 2004; Wills, 2002).

The ITF was meanwhile pursuing international collective bargaining in the shipping industry with rather more success. The 'Flags of Convenience' (FOC) campaign, initiated in the late 1940s gathered momentum in the 1960s and began to bite in the 1970s. The campaign had political and industrial thrusts, and succeeded in enforcing minimum standards of pay in many of the world's ships. We expand on the FOC campaign in Chapter five.

Towards a Unified International Movement

The existence of a common enemy helped the ICFTU to mobilise affiliates, but simultaneously illustrated the significance of the division between itself and the other confederations. The increasingly anomalous existence of Apartheid in South Africa brought the ICFTU to develop a widely supported campaign. The Confederation undoubtedly made a real contribution here, overcoming the many constraints limiting its capacity for independent action (Gumbrell-McCormick, 2001). The circumstances were quite specific, in that there was a considerable consensus among affiliates that the Confederation should act (Gumbrell-McCormick, 2001). Roger Southall (1995) has shown however that effective solidarity was still restricted because of Cold War tensions between the ICFTU, the ITSs and the (non-dues paying) WFTU affiliate, the South African Congress of Trade Unions.

As the multinationals grew in strength, and pushed at existing trade boundaries, semi-official meetings were held between officials of the world's divided trade union movement (Lieβ, 1983). The extension of Western corporations into the Comecon countries provided a motive for Western unionists to show increased interest in Eastern Europe, while the emergence of 'dissident unionism' there ironically provided a motive for official Soviet unions to shore up their role through contact with their Western counterparts (Busch, 1983).

After 1989 and the collapse of Communism, the way was paved for a more unified trade union movement at international level and extension of previously limited attempts to develop international networks and collective bargaining. Huge areas of the international economy were now opened up to companies and the ICFTU tried to take the opportunity to expand its influence. A key conclusion of a 1990 ICFTU/ITS Conference was that the ICFTU should strengthen their 'coordination of the work of the ITSs and national centres' and a new department for multinationals was established at the Confederation (ICFTU, 1990; Gumbrell-McCormick, 2000a: 514). As this showed, the ICFTU did not accept a role limited to lobbying but wished to expand its coordinating, organising and bargaining functions.

Unions in the former Soviet Union were allowed back into the fold of 'free' trade unions, even if their qualifications for entry were highly questionable. In the words of one commentator, the arrival of the ex-Soviet unions 'unleashed a tremendous struggle to remake the geography of workers' representation in central and Eastern Europe' (Herod, 2001: 224). In the 1990s, even before these unions were admitted to the ICFTU, many affiliated to GUFs. The GUFs were therefore able quickly to come into direct contact where the ICFTU could not, and this was used to reject the ICFTU's hegemonic claims within the international movement. The irony was that these unions' ultimate admission to the ICFTU entailed only limited strengthening of it, because the former Soviet Union affiliates of WFTU had no tradition of negotiating with management. The main weapon used by the internationals has been an expansion of the GUF's educational activities aimed at improving unions' capacity to represent members (Sogge, 2004).

The loss of most Russian unions, and that of a significant number of others in the world who left the WFTU without subsequently joining the ICFTU meant that WFTU withered, and stopped publishing membership figures in the 1990s although it continues to play some role in India, Latin America and the Arab countries. This left the ICFTU as by far the biggest international player, with the relatively tiny Christian WCL the only alternative.

In November 2006, the ITUC was formed from the ICFTU, the WCL and a number of sizeable and influential left-wing unions such as the Polish OPZZ, the Argentinean CTA, the Colombian CUT and the French CGT. Since the WCL's strength lay in the developing and transitional countries, the international trade union movement achieved better international coverage even though some WCL affiliates refused to join. At the same time, the ITUC established a Pan-European Council including non-ETUC unions and notably the Russians, who are not represented in the EU-oriented ETUC (Traub-Merz and Eckl, 2007).

Politically divisive tendencies persist in some of the world's unions, and the largest issue is that of the state controlled unions in the All-China Federation of Trade Unions (ACFTU), not currently recognised as free unions by the ITUC. The ACFTU is linking up with African unions through its cooperation with and funding of the Organisation of African Trade Unions and their financing of the sizeable Nkrumah Labour College in Accra (Traub-Merz and Eckl, 2007). There are voices arguing for engagement with the ACFTU through the latter's admission to the ITUC, an issue that threatens to re-divide the international free trade union movement.

Conclusion

The international movement is now closer to being worthy of the global description than ever before, and previous political and religious obstacles to unity in action that restricted attempts to deal with multinationals have been removed.

Key structural issues have been evident throughout the movement's history and continue to loom large today. Perhaps the most important is the reluctance of national unions to cede power to international organisations. Another is the respective roles of the sectoral and umbrella bodies. The importance of educational work as a central and in many respects unifying activity helping the internationals establish shared activity of value to affiliates has been evident.

Those active in the international trade union movement continue to find positive resources in their organisations' history: its sheer length demonstrates the depth of their experience. The internationals' collective record of actively resisting fascism and opposing Apartheid represent shared touchstones. While political differences may have been at the centre of the international movement's history, both sides now refer to a shared tradition of campaigning against both.

The length of the organisations' histories goes well beyond being a collective resource because it encourages affiliates to take a long-term view of their involvement and of the benefits to be gained from it, an idea we expand on in Chapter four.

II
The Work of
the Internationals

The Internationals –
Governance and Resources

All international trade union organisations face three tasks: organisation, policy, and democratisation. This means international trade union policy must be democratised, it must reach deep down among the membership, including them, involving them.

Dan Gallin, ex-general secretary of the IUF (quoted in Rütters, 2001: 1)

Introduction

THIS chapter examines the central political dynamics within the internationals. We begin with an analytical account of how they are governed, showing the developed country unions' dominance of the GUFs' structures, underpinned by their high financial contributions. We also explain the current resource difficulties and the consequent political choice that the more financially secure affiliates are now faced with.

We also argue that the two most commonly discussed strategies of merger and de-regionalisation are unlikely to deal effectively either with the GUFs' difficulties or the underlying problem of national union decline. We therefore advocate two measures. The first is an increased material contribution from more developed countries. The second, for which we draw on international relations theories, is to encourage regions and sub-regions to make a contribution themselves. We suggest that they pursue a union development agenda organised on a small group or 'minilateral' basis and seek funding to support it. We believe the latter measure offers real possibilities for accessing funds, for improving the real involvement of developing country unions in the internationals and for building the affiliated unions themselves.

We begin with an overview of the internationals' membership and explain how they are governed and staffed. Next, the resources problem is examined. Finally, we expand in detail on the two proposed measures for arresting and reversing recent trends.

Global Governance: Structures and Authority

Shown in Map 2, the GUFs' headquarters are all in Europe. Most executive and statutory (i.e. required by rule) international meetings are hosted at headquarters.

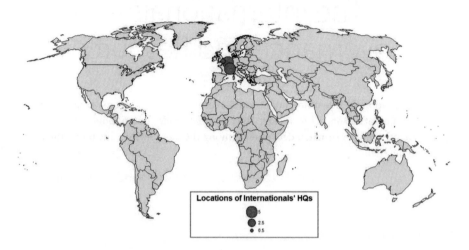

Map 2: Locations of Internationals' HQs

In 2004, the regional offices were distributed as shown in Map 3.

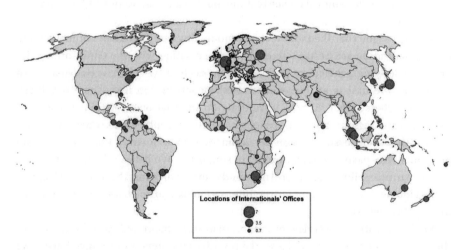

Map 3: Locations of Internationals' Offices

In addition many internationals have established technical support offices in sub-regions and specific countries, mainly to manage particular programmes and projects, shown in Map 4.

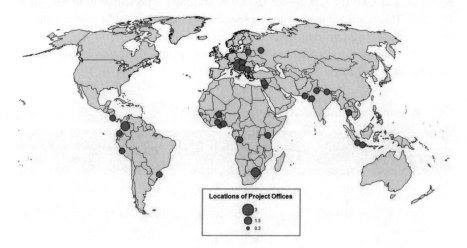

Map 4: Locations of Project Offices

The internationals, in common with other union organisations, have well-developed governance systems and all maintain strict formal decision-making procedures based on their rules or 'statutes'. These formal structures and procedures constitute a framework providing some constraints on powerful groups. The first democratising structure, also standard in national unions, is congress. Congress is the highest decision-making body, and in most cases meets every four years. This contrasts with almost all national unions where congresses are held more frequently. Congresses host around two thousand delegates and provide opportunities for unions to network and lobby for their agendas. Formal congress procedures are also tightly administered by headquarters officials, restricting the possibility of unanticipated decisions.

All internationals have dues payment categories reflecting ability to pay, with most affiliates clustered in the lower paying ones. In an attempt to limit the voting power of high-paying affiliates, voting rights are in most GUFs determined by paying membership levels regardless of category of payment. The only exception is the removal of voting rights from unions who have paid no affiliation fees. This is a second democratising measure, that seeks to de-couple subscription from participation but, significantly, voting is restricted to leadership elections and issues where consensus cannot be reached. Congresses, by virtue of their infrequency and the lack of decision-taking opportunities, therefore have very restricted possibilities for determining or affecting strategy.

The internationals' executives meet more frequently, usually annually, but in some cases twice a year. Seats are allocated for regional committee members, regional distribution and women since the internationals have all made concerted efforts over at least the last decade to ensure statutory representation of women at all levels. This is a third democratising measure. It has helped to broaden executive meeting agendas and in some cases how debate is conducted.

Table 4 shows the distribution of executive positions by region in the ICFTU between 1972 and 2003.

Table 4: Regional Distribution of Executive Positions in Relation to Membership in the ICFTU, 1972–2003

Region	1972				1983				1992				2003			
	Seats	%	Mbp	%	Seats	%	Mbp	%	Seats	%	Mbp	%	Seats	%	Mbp	%
Africa	3	12	868	2	4	11	546	1	5	11	1,997	2	6	13	10,590	9
Asia	5	20	4295	11	6	17	11,047	14	8	18	19,628	20	11	23	27,282	24
West Asia	1	3	1800	2	1	2	800	1								
Middle East	2	8	844	2	2	6	865	1	2	4	882	1	2	4	1,273	1
Latin America	3	12	1552	4	4	11	12,608	16	5	11	10,812	11	6	13	16,467	15
Caribbean	1	4	122	-	1	3	311	-	1	2	149	-	1	2	382	1
Third World	*14*	*56*	*7,681*	*20*	*18*	*51*	*27,177*	*34*	*22*	*50*	*34,268*	*35*	*26*	*55*	*55,994*	*50*
Europe	8	32	27,805	72	10	29	35,902	45	14	32	46,872	48	15	32	43,637	39
North America	2	8	1,300	3	6	17	14,902	19	6	14	14,990	15	6	13	12,362	11

Source: Gumbrell McCormick (2002) and ICFTU Congress Reports

The Table shows that in 2003 the developing country unions had a small majority of executive seats in the ICFTU. However, this tells us little about their weight in decision making both there and in GUFs. In reality, a consensus between the main unions of the developed world, and especially those that contribute high amounts financially (the Germans, Nordics, North Americans and Japanese) is likely to carry any vote.

Formal authority runs in clear lines up to the general secretary and president. General secretaries and presidents are elected officials, as opposed to the vast majority of those working for the internationals who are appointed functionaries. General secretaries are currently all European. An increasing number of presidents are from developing countries. The general secretary carries ultimate responsibility for their organisations but this is to some extent shared with presidents particularly at times of political conflict. The great majority of senior officials are men, with only one female GUF general secretary, Anita Normark of BWI.

Information is controlled and distributed by the senior officers and this group therefore has significant power to set agendas (Lukes, 2002). Officers' power in this respect probably exceeds that of union officers at national level, because of the linguistic barriers and wide range of difficult-to-interpret information involved internationally. As Kratochwil argues, there is a 'baffling' array of information requirements for players in a multilateral setting, and this is apparent in the case of the internationals. He argues that for international organisations to be able to achieve consensus and cooperation, 'of paramount importance is the interpretation of the "facts" and inferences about motivations' (Kratochwil, 1993: 448). This complex process of interpretation is inevitably dominated by permanent officials. They also play a significant role in working groups. Working groups and non-statutory committees, formed regularly to review and develop policy are the general secretary's main partners in policy making.

Executive committees are formally responsible for running the organisation between congresses. However, Kahler's (1992) problem of 'latency' is evident in these committees. 'Latency' describes the situation whereby members become passive in large diverse groups. Delegates fall into diplomatic mode and rarely raise contentious issues publicly, with the breaks and evenings providing important social and political contact. Few delegates attend executive meetings in order to help resolve difficult international issues. All delegates' unions face their own financial and political problems and delegates are reluctant to tackle the same problems multiplied at international level. In addition, they are concerned to maintain unity and there is therefore limited real participation at this level. Thus, the financial difficulties that we analyse below are little discussed even within the internationals' executives and are certainly not publicised. As a result, a subject of fundamental importance is not widely understood and is only discussed within a highly restricted group, often in informal situations. This group largely consists of officials together with the representatives of influential national unions, which is largely coterminous with those making large financial contributions.

There are three types of authority that unions can draw on in their dealings with each other in these bodies: *contribution authority, political authority* and *moral authority*. The first comes from the amount that a union is seen to contribute to the collective both in financial and human terms and has primacy over other forms of authority. Germany, USA, Canada, Japan and the Nordic region collectively represent on average 80 per cent of the internationals' dues income. High levels of affiliation fees and external project funding coming from Western European and North American unions means that the focus at executive level is on their interests, and this is well understood by unions from elsewhere. Conversely, where a region has been consistently unable to deliver appropriate affiliation fee payments, for example Latin America in recent years, their credibility and influence is much diminished.

Political authority comes from the perceived political importance of an affiliate's country and its trade union movement. At the global policy level, this is closely associated with contribution authority although the political positioning of an affiliate at important political moments is also significant in the shorter term.

The third, more temporary form of authority is moral. Moral authority is acquired when a union movement becomes prominent because of its exceptional achievements or particularly adverse environment; recent examples are Colombia and Iraq. When representatives from these countries speak they are not contradicted and in general they are supported. But this does not confer any wider authority on them to influence global strategy and therefore the authority is limited and transient.

Staffing

Some 700 people globally work for GUFs, 380 at headquarters and 297 in regional offices. This is a small number in comparison both with the ITUC and with major non-governmental organisations: in 2007, for example, Oxfam had 6,000 employees worldwide. This small staff must administer organisations which themselves consume large amounts of time and energy, with high levels of reporting and written accounting to executive bodies. The workforce's capacity to meet these demands seems likely to decline in the near future, as approximately 50 per cent of the internationals' existing staff will retire by 2013. Many of these staff have enormous understanding of particular industry sectors and unmatched in-country experience acquired over long periods, raising a serious question about the regeneration of human resources within the internationals.

Archer (2001) suggests that the national composition of staff is an important dimension for judging an organisation's degree of internationalisation. In this sense, different internationals represent variations on a theme. In some cases the general secretary strongly affects the functionaries' national make up; in others the influence of powerful affiliates dominates while in a third group both influences are combined. There are therefore high proportions of South African, German, American, Australian, Japanese and British staff.

Employment in the regions is often more precarious than at the headquarters secretariats, weakening the formers' overall position in relation to headquarters. In some GUFs, a proportion of those working in the regions is employed on temporary contracts, through externally funded projects. The number of staff employed by the internationals is provided in Table 5 below, with the minimum numbers employed on temporary contracts given in brackets.

Table 5: Numbers of Staff Employed by the Internationals, 2004

Global Union	Total Number of Head Office Staff	Regional Staff					Total Number of Regional Staff	Total Number of Union Staff	Percentage of Head Office Staff
		Africa	Americas	Asia Pacific	Europe	Middle East and North Africa			
EI	33	12	8	9	4		33	66	50
ICFTU	84	12 (2)	17 (3)	19	8 (4)	2	58 (9)	142 (9)	59
IFBWW	14	8 (6)	5 (2)	14 (8)	1 (1)	1 (1)	29 (18)	43 (18)	33
ICEM	17	2	4	2	2		10	27	63
IFJ	12 (3)	2 (1)	3 (1)	3 (1)	3		11 (3)	23 (6)	52
IMF	22	3	5	9 (4)	2		19 (4)	41 (4)	54
ITGLWF	7	3	4	4	4		15	22	32
ITF	102	5	7	10	11	1	34	136	75
IUF	19 (2)	2 (1)	7 (2)	12 (8)	12 (2)		33 (13)	52 (15)	37
PSI	28	12	9	15	20	2 (2)	58 (2)	86 (2)	33
UNI	41	8	12	10	16		46	87	47
TUAC	9 (3)							9 (3)	50
Total	388 (8)	69 (10)	81 (8)	107 (21)	83 (7)	6 (3)	346 (49)	734 (57)	Average 49

Note 1: The 'Head Office staff' figures include secretariat staff not located in Head Offices. The figures in brackets refer to the minimum numbers of staff employed on temporary contracts.
Note 2: The ICEM closed its regional offices and relocated the secretariat to Geneva during the period 2007–2008.
Source: Schwass (2004)

Outside of the developed world, externally funded projects play a considerable role in providing staff. Not all of the internationals provided current information for this table, but it gives some indication of how many staff members are partly (more than 50 per cent) or wholly financed by project funds: for example, 8 (6) means that out of 8 staff, 6 are financed by project funds. The number of staff sponsored by project funds is in reality higher than shown here since some GUFs operate numerous project offices separate from the regional offices. The proportion of head office to regional staff in the last column is calculated without taking project staff into consideration; European regional organisations independent of GUFs have also been omitted (Schwass, 2004).

The governance of the internationals therefore places considerable power in their European headquarters, whilst influence within them is concentrated in affiliates with high contribution authority. Most affiliated unions fall outside of this category.

Membership

The key task in the 1980s and 1990s was seen to be moving away from being based in the developed world and towards becoming genuinely global organisations. There was therefore an intense drive to build affiliation levels in order to permit elections to regional structures, and this proved highly effective. The internationals recruited large numbers of unions, many of which became the recipients of resources from the developed world's unions. Despite this drive, the internationals' regions today are globally incomplete, since at this point few GUFs have established presences in the Middle East and none have offered formal recognition to the Chinese unions.

Non-OECD unions' motivations for affiliating have important consequences. According to Logue (1980), strong national unions will only affiliate to international bodies if they cannot solve their problems at national level; in the case of non-OECD unions, the converse applied since many of the unions affiliating were not and had never been strong. They affiliated because they were weak. Some sought to substitute for old alliances that had previously sustained them. African and Asian unions involved in national liberation movements had seen an erosion of their previously close relationships with the nationalists in power after independence and started to experience pressures to subordinate themselves to states (Wood and Brewster, 2007). Others saw affiliation as a step out of political and industrial isolation. For many unions, joining the internationals was their first opportunity to build genuinely global contacts on the basis of relative equality, as previously international contacts had been with ex-colonising countries' unions. They were in addition often controlled by national political élites. For other unions, such as those from the former Soviet Union, affiliation was seen as a way of affirming their democratic legitimacy by gaining admission to the free trade union movement. It also provided them with a way of looking at other forms of unionism which they had not been able to access before the 1990s, without committing themselves to adopting any of them.

These motivations sustained unions through affiliation processes which they experienced as difficult and involved them in divulging organisational information that they would have preferred not to submit. In the case of the ITUC, affiliation was also a protracted process as it maintained a now-abandoned policy of limiting affiliations to one per country, and in many countries competing union structures and political affiliations made selection processes lengthy. These processes raised expectations of what could be delivered after affiliation, and in many cases the demands overwhelmed the internationals. The real possibilities of providing help were dwarfed by the expectations of unions whose only previous experiences of international organisations were of large bodies such as the United Nations or well-resourced NGOs.

Some unions, such as those based in South Africa, were relatively self-sufficient, but these were a small minority. Most new affiliates posed major difficulties, and foremost among them were those from the former Soviet Union. Since the 1990s, these unions have put significant pressure on the GUFs to help them become more effective organisations. Most of these vast unions, with formal memberships numbering millions, were completely unknown to the internationals, since they had previously been excluded from the ITUC 'family'. They are heterogeneous and virtually impossible accurately to map (Garver et al., 2007). Whilst making demands on the internationals, they maintain their old affiliations. The VKP, the CIS regional structure dating from Soviet times, continues to operate and to provide an alternative locus of activity, and, along with WFTU, in the 1990s opposed national union affiliation to the Western 'anti-communist' internationals. In 2000 the Russian FNPR affiliated to the ICFTU. However, its President, Mikhail Shmakov, currently sits as the President of VKP, highlighting the Russian unions' decision to live in both worlds. The GUFs were aware of the Russian stance and unions were usually admitted to GUFs without any serious pressure being put on them to reform prior to admission. These unions therefore posed real challenges when they came into the internationals as full members.

The Chinese unions, whose formal membership is in excess of the rest of the world put together, represent a further responsibility for the internationals. Most GUFs conduct 'active engagement', which entails forming diplomatic and in some cases technical relations without discussing affiliation. In this case, they receive no income for their work.

The recently affiliated unions are the main beneficiaries of the transfer of resources that occurs within the internationals, and developed country unions have to justify that transfer to their own members. In the next chapters we look at two of the most significant areas of activity for European and North American unions: collective bargaining and networking across multinationals. Here is an important positive argument for their contributions, because international bargaining and networking are easily identifiable products. National networking between affiliates of the same GUF is a further benefit. Less-apparent benefits also exist, including being able to call on the internationals' experience and linking capacities. It is often assumed that it is only the developing country membership which either needs this level of support or can demand it from other affiliates. Yet many cases exist of OECD country unions benefiting from international support during disputes. One recent example is that of the powerful Finnish Paper Workers' Union which in 2005 received extensive support from many unions including the Brazilian paper workers in its successful battle to resist employers' attempts to increase the use of contract labour.

In summary, the internationals have faced increased demands from their affiliates outside of the developed world for which they receive little income, and although identifiable benefits exist for OECD-based affiliates, this has caused them to examine their commitment more closely.

Headquarters–Regions Relations

There is clearly a balance to be struck between the requirement to tailor policies and practices to specific conditions on the one hand and the need to ensure coherence in global policies and activities on the other.

The issue is strongly affected by broader political attitudes. Sentiment in favour of increased regional autonomy has solid underpinnings, both in Europe and in the developing world, where unions have long been suspicious of the 'imperialist' foundations of the global unions. This is especially apparent in radical unions in Latin America who see the Western European and North American domination of the international structures as reflecting the policies of their national governments, and as part of an imperialist policy. These broad sentiments are shared by many other unions in the developing world.

Gumbrell-McCormick, in her study of the ICFTU, approaches the centre–region balance issue through the concept of federalism, defined as 'individuals gathering together through national groups to act in common with other national groups' (2001: 20). Strong and weak federalism are distinguished, depending on the level of power delegated by national unions to the internationals. In the ICFTU, federalism is relatively strong because regions are virtually autonomous. Regional structures within GUFs have varying degrees of autonomy but federalism is weak in the majority because regions are essentially subordinated to the headquarters. Most are effectively outposts of the international and are, unlike the ITUC's regions, not regarded as essentially autonomous organisations.

Regional executive committees generally meet twice a year and regional conferences are held, in the main, every four years, putting considerable power in the hands of regional officials. Regional secretaries head regional offices, and they are usually appointed functionaries of the international. In these cases the GUF exercises control through its regional secretary. In a minority of cases (the ITUC, UNI and IUF) the equivalent officer is elected, with the title of regional general secretary. In simple terms the distinction is between a regional secretary, whose job is to represent the interests of the international within the region, and a regional general secretary or elected regional president, whose task is to represent the interests of the region to the international executive.

Regional autonomy is also limited because, for the majority of GUFs, budgetary and financial issues are ultimately regulated exclusively at headquarters level. In recent years, internal and external auditors have begun to focus on the regions' financial practices, bringing criticism of the management of project funds and standards of accountability more widely. They also refer to the precarious position of regional offices and structures, and in particular the common problem of the non-registration and lack of legal standing of regional offices and structures with national authorities.

Regions are further weakened in relation to headquarters by the distribution of authority within the regions themselves, since they are not homogenous blocs of countries with shared interests. Within each region, with the exception of Western Europe, clear national centres of influence exist. In Africa, South African unions dominate, providing up to 80 per cent of GUFs' regional income. They are a much admired union movement that emerged through struggle, an evolution not replicated by unions in other African nations. They therefore combine a high degree of all three of the types of authority identified above. The South African unions are, on the other hand, self-conscious in their dominance of political processes, a self-consciousness that is not evident in the cases of Japan in Asia and the USA in the Americas. In Asia, Japanese unions exert strong influence on the basis of high contribution authority. In Latin America, despite the fragmentation of the organisations themselves, the Brazilian unions do likewise through political authority. Where structures cover the Americas, the North American unions essentially control them through a combination of contribution and political authority. In Eastern Europe, Russian unions are highly influential, also through contribution and political authority. In Western Europe, power relations between countries are more balanced. The Nordic unions are well interconnected and tend towards common positions that increase their influence within the European and international structures. They, along with the Germans, in most cases the highest dues payers to international bodies, are also the main funders of international projects and that contribution authority, although not always decisive, gives their views heavy weighting in GUFs.

As implied above, a different centre–periphery model exists in the ITUC and some GUFs, closer to a strong federalist arrangement where regional structures enjoy high levels of autonomy. The most extreme example is the ITUC, which has the powerful European TUC and three autonomous regional organisations (Africa, Asia and Latin America).

However, analysis using the federalist concept only takes us so far. It focuses on centre–affiliate relations and therefore does not help greatly in addressing the issue of imbalances of influence within and between regions. The imbalances issue is important because it limits many unions' influence, involvement and commitment.

The concept of multilateralism, which focuses on coordinated relations beyond those of the centre and affiliates, is useful here. The GUFs are multilateral bodies; their multilateralism contains federalism. In other words, multilateralism forms an outer frame for federalism. Ruggie defines multilateralism as it applies to norms, régimes and organisations as follows:

Multilateralism is an institutional form that coordinates relations among three or more states on the basis of generalized principles of conduct; that is, principles which specify appropriate conduct for a class of actions, without regard to the particularist interests of the parties or the strategic exigencies that may exist in any specific occurrence.

(Ruggie, 1993: 77)

Axelrod and Keohane's (1986) idea of 'diffuse reciprocity', where membership of a multilateral organisation is expected to yield a rough equivalence of benefits between members in the aggregate and over time, usefully deepens Ruggie's multilateralism concept. The multilateralism and diffuse reciprocity of GUF membership contrasts with the bilateralism and short-lived nature of an increasing amount of international union work. Bilateralism is both particularist and linked to a particular situation such as a campaign; it is normally a short-term relationship based on specific reciprocity. Diffuse reciprocity on the other hand is longer term, in that affiliates do not expect short-term payoffs from their membership.

Ruggie (1993) argues that multilateral structures are sustainable because the generalised organising principles on which they are based are more elastic than those of bilateral relationships. This elasticity means that multilaterals are able to contain internal tensions, especially when their work is in demand. The theory helps explain the GUFs' immense adaptability, and even their survival in a context of extreme resource pressures.

Multilateralism, as we suggested above, provides a flexible outer frame for federal arrangements and for groupings of different sorts. These internal small groups, with the right incentives, are able to work towards creating collective goods. As Olson says:

If the central or federated organization provides some service to the small constituent organizations, they may be induced to use their social incentives to get the individuals belonging to each small group to contribute toward the achievement of the collective goals of the whole group.

(Olson, 1965: 62)

In short, multilateralist bodies like the GUFs can contain smaller or 'minilateral' (Kahler, 1992) groupings that can strengthen them. This is positive both because of the problem of 'latency' and due to the power imbalances within GUFs and their regions. We return to this later, since it has a bearing on the resource issue which we now outline.

The Resource Issue

Developed country unions are experiencing a steady decline in the number of workers paying subscriptions. Table 6 shows how this is reflected in the ICFTU through the declining numbers of members that national unions actually pay subscriptions for in relation to their declared membership.

In 2001 the ICFTU claimed 147 million members (the WCL estimated its membership at 4.3 million at that time). These figures are only broadly indicative, since they include over 50 per cent of unions implausibly declaring exactly the same membership figures for each year over a five- or six-year period (ICFTU, 2001b).

Falling membership in the majority of unions has a direct and dramatic effect on the internationals' dues income, a key source of funding. Only one per cent of union membership dues worldwide is dedicated to international action and affiliation. The most recent calculation of the funds available to the internationals, carried out as part of the ITUC's Millennium Review in 2001, estimated a total income of US$60 million per year from membership dues, donated funds and development cooperation funds raised externally. Between 1999 and 2003, an additional US$70 million of donations and project funds was channelled through ITUC regional structures. To put these figures in comparative perspective, Oxfam received some US$580 million in 2007, while the British union Unite claimed an income in the same year equivalent to about US$400 million.

Table 6: ICFTU Declared and Paying Membership by Region, 1998 and 2003

Region	1998		2003	
	Declared Membership	Paying Membership	Declared Membership	Paying Membership
Western Europe	43,214,250	37,594,584	43,637,707	36,233,803
Asia and Pacific	27,907,407	18,112,000	27,282,638	14,708,392
Latin America	19,361,761	19,254,000	16,467,678	7,439,380
North America	14,612,112	14,612,112	12,362,956	12,362,056
Africa	8,941,858	8,454,000	10,590,676	10,254,425
Central and Eastern Europe/ N.I.S.	8,235,265	8,048,000	37,296,378	11,300,583
Middle East	747,800	745,000	1,273,528	1,271,000
West Indies	420,332	424,122	382,798	387,000
Totals	**123,440,785**	**107,243,818**	**149,294,359**	**93,956,639**
Percentage of membership for which dues paid	87		63	

Source: ICFTU (2004) and authors' calculations

The 2001 analysis noted that real value fee receipts per member had dropped by 22 per cent since 1994 (ICFTU, 2001a). Table 7 shows the actual fees received from its affiliates in 1998 and 2003. Between 1999 and 2003 the ICFTU increased its membership by 28 million but saw a fall in paying membership of 12.4 per cent. In addition, the internationals all face a serious challenge from the late payment of membership fees.

Table 7: ICFTU Actual Fees Received per Region, 1998 and 2003

Region	Actual Fees Received, 1998 (EURO)	Actual Fees Received, 2003 (EURO)	Percentage Change (+ or -)
Central and Eastern Europe/N.I.S.	115,884	194,870	+68.2
West Indies	3,030	4,351	+43.6
Western Europe	5,403,298	5,862,541	+8.5
North America	2,215,906	1,647,439	-25.7
Africa	131,899	67,675	-48.7
Asia and Pacific	1,467,920	490,412	-66.6
Latin America	29,744	4,259	-85.7
Middle East	37,890	5,155	-86.4

Source: ICFTU (2004)

National unions practise trade-offs between affiliation fees and the number of members they choose to affiliate: if the international increases fees, they simply reduce the number of members affiliated. The internationals' resources are therefore strictly limited by the amounts that national unions are prepared to contribute, conceived of in essentially historic terms. In 2004–5, the ICEM tried to address the problem directly in an explicit but unsuccessful attempt to raise international affiliation fees higher on the political agenda of OECD country unions. Annual accounts revealed that a 2003 affiliation fee increase, designed to bring a 14.29 per cent increase in income brought only a 1.2 per cent increase in 2004 (ICEM, 2004a; ICEM, 2004b). Here was explicit confirmation of the GUFs' previous experience, that raising affiliation fee levels simply leads to a reduction in claimed membership by affiliates. The ICEM discussed two alternative responses. Initially, it considered presenting the case for affiliates to devote an increased percentage of their national income to international work. After enormous and at times acrimonious debate amongst affiliates at international and regional levels, this proposal was rejected as unrealistic. Affiliates were unable to secure sufficient political support within their own organisations to defend an increase in affiliation fee levels. The only remaining option was to reduce expenditure and to close regional offices. The ICEM's regions have from then on been assisted by the secretariat.

Project funding is also essential income, used to sustain educational activities that, as we outline in Chapter seven, are considerable. In total, project funding represented just under half of the internationals' total income in 2000 (ICFTU, 2001f). Increasingly, the internationals blur the line between project activity and the resource people employed to manage them on the one hand, and their core costs and staff on the other. Schwass (2004: 22) refers to this blurring in diplomatic terms: 'the term "direct project costs" is somewhat difficult to define'. It is therefore impossible precisely to estimate the balance between membership dues and project funding, a particular issue in the cases of the ITGLWF, BWI and ITUC. The area is sensitive since it is clear that a sizeable proportion of the internationals' funds come from outside the trade union movement. This fundamental reality, which has gone un-noticed or at least un-mentioned by other authors, is a major issue. It clearly means that the internationals are dependent on external funders and risk becoming essentially project-driven organisations as happened to the IFPAAW prior to its forced merger with the IUF in 1994. There is a need for the international trade union movement to become less dependent on these sources.

Nevertheless, the internationals' ability to continue to raise significant project funds currently remains crucial. Potential exists here to develop the role of GUF regions, since donors have increasingly decentralised arrangements, with funding decisions often being made at regional and sub-regional levels. Those GUFs with a relatively strong federalism may therefore have a potential route out of financial problems, especially when combined with a minilateral approach where several countries' unions collaborate. GUF regions operating within a strong federalist model, such as the IUF's East European region, have already been able to use their independence to raise considerable project funds.

Financial problems have intensified debate over the appropriate level of regional autonomy. In this debate, the case advanced by headquarters for improved regional accountability cannot be dismissed as simply a device for headquarters to increase their specific weight. In the ITUC's 2004 Congress documents, the financial auditors complained of a lack of consistent financial reporting from AFRO (ITUC, 2004). Gottfurcht had done the same in 1966, indicating that this is a long-term issue and not one invented opportunistically.

Thus, the financial problem means that the internationals rely heavily on external funding to support key areas of activity. An answer may lie in more rather than less regional autonomy, but regional accountability both upwards and downwards remains an issue. These, however, are not the terms in which the internationals' future is normally discussed.

Re-structuring the Internationals

The most recent major attempt to generate discussion around restructuring, the ITUC's Millennium Review, failed seriously to involve GUF executives and brought only minor results disproportionate to the scale of the problems.

Within the internationals, discussion of organisational strategy focuses almost entirely on a merger of the main GUFs. One GUF, the ITGLWF, clearly has inadequate resources to carry out the range of tasks required of any global union body, and merger offers a way out which it intends to take. For other GUFs, pushing the merger trend to its logical conclusion is not a solution that will be widely acceptable; some, like the IUF, have set policies firmly against merger. A common suggestion (see for example Traub-Merz and Eckl, 2007) is to establish two large GUFs, one for manufacturing and one for the public sector. However, the current prospects of the GUFs agreeing to merger on this scale are tiny. There are several understandable reasons for this. First, GUF merger has invariably meant that one headquarters has to be chosen, bringing the loss of uniquely experienced staff. Second, some international trade unionists refer to the national level experience of merger which has often entailed long periods of internal disruption. There is some support from serious research for that viewpoint (Dempsey, 2004), and it was long ago suggested that mergers fail to overcome the problems that create them (Chaison, 1996). It seems that although no research exists on GUF mergers, these problems are likely only to be magnified at international level. Third, it is pointed out that many of the claimed benefits of GUF merger centre on cost reductions that are not assured or quantified, and that could be obtained in other ways.

In 2006, in direct response to the weakness of the solutions under discussion, the Council of Global Unions was formed to intensify coordination and cooperation. Yet this appears to have attracted little support from several GUFs, with the IUF and IMF deciding not to participate. The objection is that it is, in the words of one official, 'a complete waste of scarce resources'. Currently, neither merger nor the Council of Global Unions offer viable solutions to the current resource problems.

Prior to discussing a proposed solution, we note that the internationals stand to benefit from a management review encompassing all of them, similar to those that have been carried out by some trade union movements at national level (for a review and comparison of these in Canada, the USA and Britain, see Clark et al., 1998). At a minimum, this seems likely at least to make useful suggestions as to how efficiency could be improved both individually and collectively. Some of the issues to be covered, such as succession planning for the high proportion of staff due to retire over the next decade, are especially urgent.

Small Groups: Collaboration and Minilateralism

In the current situation, a further strategic review seems unlikely to attract sufficient support from the GUFs to be viable; the Millennium Review may be read as an illustration of the intractability of the structural issues. We now outline an alternative approach.

Both research and experience indicate that small groups are able to work more effectively together and deliver improvements to the internationals' work even with reduced income. We therefore suggest a move away from a merger/restructuring focus and towards increased inter- and intra-GUF collaboration.

Intra-GUF collaboration can be enhanced by small groups of unions working closely together on concrete issues, offering the prospect of overcoming Kahler's problem of 'latency'. Small groups create environments where individuals and individual organisations are more likely to form robust relationships. They find it easier to define their own individual and collective interests and to navigate the process of forming alliances and working with other organisations. When small groups are comprised of geographically, politically or industrially connected unions there is potential for them to operate effectively together in symbiotic ways.

There are two ways in which small groups can make international groupings more effective, as described by Kahler (1992); in one, the group acts as a 'broker' (sometimes described in practice as 'missionaries') for negotiations within the wider grouping. In the other, the small group operates as a 'progressive club' in which it develops and promotes more progressive policies or work than the 'lowest common denominator' normally experienced in larger groups. This model offers global unions a way of developing meaningful and ambitious collaboration between affiliates.

A strategic approach to inter-GUF collaboration could also be usefully developed by substantially expanding a number of existing collaborations. Educational collaboration offers good prospects here. One positive example has been the ten years of GUF cooperation in the former Soviet Union across various educational programmes. A second is the work of UNI, IUF and PSI on the shared concern of private equity. The joint initiative started in 2007 and includes research and online information, with potential for joint campaigning. A third joint initiative relates to contract labour, initiated by the ICEM but being extended to include all GUFs and the ITUC. The programme has developed research and strategic discussion about how unions manage the issue in different sectors. An important element has been to spread awareness amongst unions that the growth of the use of contract labour or the 'externalisation' of work is a major threat to labour standards at local and international levels. This collaboration could involve an important campaigning (including around multinational labour agencies) and lobbying element, to relate to the current wider discussion around international labour standards. Collective bargaining provides a fourth case. The joint signing of IFAs is important for strengthening IFA credibility with stakeholders. Three currently exist and it appears likely that more will follow. Finally, significant collaboration exists between the internationals in the Middle East and North Africa, and China. The needs of both areas far outweigh the resources available, underlining the need to pool resources.

These collaborations offer global unions a focused and decentralised way of forming stronger international structures, and could provide a more ambitious and realistic way out of the current impasse.

Conclusion

The internationals have been victims of their own success in recruiting affiliates, but the influence of the latter remains limited. This is important background to the shortcomings in using international agreements and building company networks that we identify in the following chapters.

Resources have been a resilient, long-term problem. In a 'big picture' sense, the resources issue would have been recognisable to Gottfurcht in the 1960s and even to Fimmen in the post-First World War years. The reluctance of unions at national level to cede increased resources to the internationals is a long-term one that can only be addressed by a combination of the objective logic of globalisation and the political will to take the necessary steps in response.

The immediate resource issue that the internationals face can only be dealt with by developed country affiliates because it is urgent. Survival rests on this small group of unions making the political choice to devote a higher percentage of their income towards international structures than they have historically done. A strategy to convince their own executive bodies to do this when their own membership income is in decline is needed and one of this book's objectives is to provide material for such intelligent appeals to members.

There is a second, longer-term prong to our proposed strategy. We propose a minilateral approach within the existing multilateral structures. We suggest pursuing the union developmental agenda through educational activity supported by fundraising, by building sub-regional and small group programmes both between unions and the internationals themselves. Funding is increasingly decentralised and offers real opportunities for such groups. The inter-union collaboration should mobilise the demonstrated democratising effects of educational activity discussed in Chapter seven. Participation can be raised, and this can combine with increased contribution authority, providing an opportunity for developing country unions to increase their influence in the internationals.

CHAPTER FIVE

International Collective Bargaining

Two leaders of the union Edegel in Peru's electricity sector, organising workers in the Endesa group attended the ICEM project's education, which led to a number of achievements. Their improved bargaining skills directly brought better salaries and conditions of work. It helped establish a Contract Workers' Union in the company. Membership increased, so did links with the community and a library was set up for members. The International Framework Agreement with Endesa was used to improve health and safety standards, and this also included extension of the same standards to contract workers.

Cristhian Rivas, ICEM Project Coordinator Peru

Introduction

THIS chapter deals with the main tools currently used by GUFs to improve unions' ability to bargain and organise within multinationals: International Framework Agreements (IFAs).

A good deal of attention has been focussed on these agreements both within the internationals and by academics interested in the development of an international system of industrial relations (for example, ICFTU, 2001b; Wills, 2004; Müller and Rüb, 2005). They have been adopted as a major part of the industrial GUFs' strategies; UNI, IMF, ICEM, BWI, IUF and ITGLWF have all passed congress and executive resolutions to this effect. Essentially statements of fundamental rights, these agreements offer some possibilities for local unionists by establishing a context for unions to develop local bargaining with employers.

Our argument is as follows: current ways of working do not maximise IFAs' potential. Many agreements are negotiated without the involvement of unionists from developing country unions, who are not made fully aware of the agreements' purpose, ramifications and implications. Indeed, in some cases the GUFs, as the representatives of these unions, are themselves only marginally and formally involved in concluding them. Trade unions from outside of the developed world are often little involved in IFA monitoring and review processes. In these circumstances the agreements frequently do not enable developing country unions to conduct dialogue with companies. There is therefore a need to review how they are negotiated, promoted, monitored and reviewed.

Negotiating International Framework Agreements

International Framework Agreements are often concluded between unions and GUFs on the one hand and senior management on the other. We reproduce the building workers' model framework agreement in Annex 1 and an actual agreement with the French company Lafarge in Annex 2. These agreements may be seen as an attempt to establish stable relationships with companies on an international basis and they are favoured by European unions over the more adversarial and episodic US strategic campaigning approach, which identifies and attacks companies' key relationships (Russo, 1999; Greven, 2003; 2006; 2008).

IFAs may also be viewed as alternatives or supplements to unilateral company codes of conduct as, unlike these codes, they are negotiated and normally feature key union rights (Holdcroft, 2006). In some sectors, such as clothing and textiles, thousands of unilateral codes remain in existence and are likely to remain the predominant tool available to GUFs to exert leverage on companies because of union weakness. Table 8 below provides those details which we have been able to establish of the IFAs in existence in mid 2008.

Table 8: International Framework Agreements, Mid-2008

Company	Employees	Headquarters Country	Industry	GUF	Year Con- cluded	Signed by HQ Country Union
Danone	76,000 (2007)	France	Food Processing	IUF	1988	No
Accor	170,000 (2006)	France	Hotels	IUF	1995	No
IKEA	118,000 (2007)	Sweden	Furniture	BWI	1998	No
Statoil	29,500 (2007)	Norway	Oil	ICEM	1998	Yes
Faber-Castell	5,500 (2002)	Germany	Office Material	BWI	1999	Yes
Metro	208,600 (2006)	Germany	Commerce	UNI	1999	
Freudenberg	32,000 (2004)	Germany	Chemicals	ICEM	2000	Yes
Hochtief	46,800 (2006)	Germany	Construction	BWI	2000	Yes
Carrefour	456,200 (2006)	France	Retail	UNI	2001	No
Chiquita	24,000 (2007)	USA	Agriculture	IUF	2001	No

Company	Employees	Headquarters Country	Industry	GUF	Year Con-cluded	Signed by HQ Country Union
OTE Telecom	Data not available	Greece	Telecommunications	UNI	2001	Yes
Skanska	56,000 (2006)	Sweden	Construction	BWI	2001	No
Telefonica	248,400 (2007)	Spain	Telecommunications	UNI	2001	Yes
AngloGold	64,000 (2005)	South Africa	Mining	ICEM	2002	Yes
Ballast Nedam	3,700 (2006)	Netherlands	Construction	BWI	2002	Yes
DaimlerChrysler	272,300 (2007)	Germany	Auto Industry	IMF	2002	No
Endesa	27,200 (2005)	Spain	Power Industry	ICEM	2002	Yes
ENI	75,800 (2007)	Italy	Energy	ICEM	2002	Yes
Fonterra	Data not available	New Zealand	Dairy Industry	IUF	2002	Yes
Merloni	17,300 (2005)	Italy	Metal Industry	IMF	2002	Yes
Norske Skog	8,000 (2006)	Norway	Paper	ICEM	2002	Yes
Volkswagen	328,600 (2006)	Germany	Auto Industry	IMF	2002	No
GEA	19,200 (2006)	Germany	Engineering	IMF	2003	No
ISS	391,400 (2004)	Denmark	Building Cleaning	UNI	2003	Yes
Leoni	34,000 (2006)	Germany	Electrical/Automotive	IMF	2003	No
Rheinmetall	19,100 (2007)	Germany	Defence/Electronics	IMF	2003	No
SKF	38,700 (2003)	Sweden	Ball Bearing	IMF	2003	No
Bosch	Data not available	Germany	Automotive/ Electronics	IMF	2004	No
H&M	40,300 (2006)	Sweden	Retail	UNI	2004	Yes
Lukoil	148,600 (2006)	Russia	Energy	ICEM	2004	Yes
Prym	Data not available	Germany	Metal manufacturing	IMF	2004	No
Renault	128,900 (2006)	France	Auto Industry	IMF	2004	Yes
Röchling	Data not available	Germany	Engineering	IMF	2004	No
SCA	50,400 (2007)	Sweden	Paper Industry	ICEM	2004	Yes
Arcelor	320,000 (2006)	Luxembourg	Metals	IMF	2005	No
BMW	107,500 (2007)	Germany	Auto	IMF	2005	No
EADS	116,800 (2006)	Netherlands	Defence	IMF	2005	No
EDF	156,500 (2006)	France	Energy	ICEM & PSI	2005	Yes

Company	Employees	Headquarters Country	Industry	GUF	Year Con-cluded	Signed by HQ Country Union
Falck	11,300 (2004)	Denmark	Graphical	UNI	2005	
Impregilo	10,100 (2005)	Italy	Construction	BWI	2005	Yes
Lafarge	71,000 (2006)	France	Construction	BWI & ICEM	2005	No
Rhodia	17,000 (2006)	France	Chemicals	ICEM	2005	Yes
Stabilo	Data not available	Germany	Cosmetics/ Instruments	BWI	2005	Yes
Veidekke	6,300 (2006)	Norway	Construction	BWI	2005	Yes
Euradius	Data not available	Netherlands	Graphical	UNI	2006	Yes
Nampak	Data not available	South Africa	Graphical	UNI	2006	No
Portugal Telecom	32,300 (2005)	Portugal	Telecoms	UNI	2006	Yes
PSA Peugeot Citroen	211,700 (2006)	France	Auto	IMF	2006	Yes
Royal BAM	30,300 (2006)	Netherlands	Construction	BWI	2006	No
Securitas	215,000 (2006)	Sweden	Property Services	UNI	2006	Yes
Staedtler	Data not available	Germany	Writing and Drafting	BWI	2006	Yes
France Telecom	187,300 (2007)	France	Telecoms	UNI	2007	Yes
Inditex	47,000	Spain	Textiles	ITGLWF	2007	No
NAG	Data not available	Australia	Finance	UNI	2007	Yes
Quebecor	43,000 (2006)	Canada	Graphical	UNI	2007	Yes
RAG	93,600 (2004)	Germany	Mining	ICEM	2007	Yes
VolkerWessels	16,600 (2004)	Netherlands	Construction	BWI	2007	No
Waz Group	Not Known	Germany	Media/journalism	IFJ	2007	No
Brunel	6,100 (2006)	Netherlands	Recruitment & and Services	IMF	2008	No
UMICORE	10,500 (2006)	Belgium	Metals	ICEM & IMF	2008	Yes
Vallourec	17,200 (2005)	France	Metals	IMF	2008	Yes

Source: IFAs taken from GUF websites, employee figures taken from Hoovers.com

IFAs originated in the late 1980s, but have developed significant momentum in the twenty-first century. They are arguably an historic breakthrough since earlier attempts at international collective bargaining in the 1960s and 1970s essentially failed (Bendiner, 1987; Rehfeldt, 1993). One reason for their emergence is that subsequent long-running attempts since the early 1970s by the ITUC and GUFs to win a social clause in international trade agreements had met with little success over the following quarter of a century. The ITUC, while claiming some success in dealings with the World Bank, acknowledged the difficulties and limitations of discussions with the international institutions (ITUC, 2006).

GUFs therefore decided at the turn of the century to try to use the Core Labour Standards that had been recently agreed by the ILO. It was thought best initially to target 'softer' European companies with requests for them to publicly accept these standards and adopt them as their own. It was seen as important to obtain a sufficient number of agreements to build momentum and to encourage more reluctant companies to start negotiations – and this proved successful. IFAs often contain statements of the ILO's Core Labour Standards, some form of review and complaints process, a communication/monitoring mechanism (generally an annual meeting between the signatories) and provision for review and re-negotiation. In 2000 just nine signed agreements existed but by 2004 there were thirty-two, and by mid-2008 sixty-one, mainly in the metalworking, chemical and energy, building and wood, and services sectors (cf. Schömann et al., 2008).

The current context is, however, not conducive to strong agreements at international level. Rehfeldt's (1993) argument in relation to the earlier international collective bargaining attempts – i.e. that they were undermined because no adequate legal framework existed for them – remains valid. Nor are current power relations conducive to negotiated compromises weighted towards workers' interests. Management are not responding to sustained pressure from workers throughout companies when they conclude IFAs (Thorpe and Mather, 2005). Company motives for reaching them are little studied, but IFAs' titles reveal a CSR agenda. For those who look no further (for example, unions outside of those involved in negotiating them) they may appear from these headings as nothing more than company CSR statements. There is a clear risk for the GUFs of being used by companies simply as accomplices in their PR efforts.

It has been argued that companies signing these agreements wish to influence stock market views of their company, develop their corporate cultures internationally, improve conflict resolution and to extend existing cooperative relations with headquarters unions (Schömann et al., 2008). The first IFA was signed by the IUF with Danone, a company that sees itself as a 'social business', a self-image it continues to develop. In this case, the image appears to have some substance. Bruno Vannoni of the IUF was quoted in 2003 as saying: 'We have a real dialogue with the company and they appear to be much more interested than many other farm-produce multinationals in listening to the concerns of employees' (Blyth, 2003: 2). Danone's family-friendly brand image as a food company also gives it sizeable exposure to the risk of costly brand damage. The majority of its workforce is employed outside of France and it is therefore exposed to the risk that its labour practices may contain pockets of poor practice.

The process of forming a relationship with management leading to an agreement is not uniform. Headquarters unions and related European Works Councils generally play an important role, but agreements are also initiated directly by GUFs (Hammer, 2005). GUFs are the only representatives of unions from outside Europe involved in negotiating IFAs and have attempted to define their role in relation to headquarters unions in concluding them. The International Metalworkers' Federation report on IFAs summarises the principles of negotiation required by that GUF. These include: reference to the ILO Core Labour Standards, universal coverage across all company operations and the importance of home country unions' and works councils' involvement in the negotiation process. The emphasis is therefore on the role of the headquarters union and works councils, reflecting the especially strong influence of powerful national unions in the engineering industry and therefore in that GUF.

The metalworkers are a specific case where workplace organisation is strong and unions are especially reluctant to delegate negotiations to the GUF. Consequently, the IMF has had little role in negotiating many of these agreements, but has often been used to sign them after they have been agreed. Thus, for example, the Röchling 'Principles of social responsibility' are signed by the company chairperson and his counterpart from the European Works Council (Ernst Gräber, also chair of the German Works Council), while two representatives of the European metalworkers and one of the IMF are described as 'entering into the agreement at the time of its signing'. Similarly, the Rheinmetall 'Principles of social responsibility' are signed by the chairperson of the European Works Council, Erik Merks, also chair of a Rheinmetall Works Council and in 2002 a member of the company's supervisory board. This agreement is signed by Merks, and also by representatives of the European metalworkers and the IMF, both of whom are described as 'joining the agreement at the time of signing' [sic]. In terms of the right to freedom of association, both agreements' texts are rather ambivalent, and refer to works council forms of representation as a legitimate alternative to trade unionism. In these cases, it appears that the chairpersons of the European Works Councils are also prominent in their German companies. The general impression is that the influence of the German headquarters union has been more significant than that of the GUF.

Other GUFs have equivalent well-organised unions within them and also experience a similar if less sharply posed issue of the balance between the global union and powerful affiliates. There are often practical reasons making it difficult for unions from developing countries to be involved in negotiations. Thus, without real GUF involvement, there is no voice in the negotiation process for unions from outside Europe. This increases the need to make these unions fully aware of the rationale for the agreement and how they might use it.

What occurs in the period after an agreement has been signed has a great bearing on whether it is used by local unions. Agreements have to be translated into all the relevant languages and sent to local management and unions. However, even if this is carried out effectively, the local representatives' level of understanding of the agreement's purpose is unlikely to be high if they simply receive a copy of the IFA without further explanation or discussion regarding the thinking behind it. Even the full meaning and import of specific terms can be an issue. For example, the term 'freedom of association' may not be immediately clear to many workers. Thorough reporting back to extra-European unions on the purpose and course of the negotiations is clearly required.

The evidence of these agreements being used to good effect in practice is not especially strong. Although the texts are often available on GUFs' websites, examples of their practical use are not prominent either there or in their publications. We surveyed selected GUF websites and publications for a six-month period, searching for such references; the results are presented in Table 9.

Table 9: References to International Framework Agreements in Selected GUF Publications

Global Union	Total Number of Items	Total Number of References to IFAs
BWI	115	1
IMF	55	10
IUF	47	0
UNI	81	3

Sources: Global Union online Newsletters & Bulletins July December 2007

The nature and purpose of IFAs could play a significant part in union educational programmes. Yet, mainly concerned with their relationships with well-organised and large European headquarters unions, GUFs currently promote them in a way that contributes little to educating or building their other affiliates' capacities. In reality, GUFs and headquarters unions substitute for the weakness of many affiliates in relation to multinationals by negotiating and signing international agreements that leave local power relationships and dynamics intact.

International Collective Bargaining: Scope and Content

Hammer (2005) distinguishes between two types of IFAs, dividing them into 'rights' and 'bargaining' agreements, with the first covering union rights and the second dealing with substantive issues. In some cases they include clauses on bargaining subjects such as health and safety and HIV/AIDS. However, the second category's title is potentially misleading: it should not be understood as *substantive bargaining on central distributive issues*, since this is not included in IFAs.

The only GUF which negotiates substantively on key distributive issues is the International Transport Workers' Federation. The ITF bargains for seafarers with groups of ship managers and employers centred on the International Maritime Employers' Committee, with whom it reaches collective agreements through the International Bargaining Forum. These managers and employers have been forced to react collectively to union power in a way that other employers currently are not (Anner et al., 2006). The ITF's long-term Flags of Convenience (FoC) campaign underpins this bargaining by establishing and enforcing conditions of employment through mobilising the combined industrial strength of seafarers, dockers and transport workers. Ships docking in well-unionised ports may be subject to industrial pressure from these groups of workers, and agreements are backed up by an international system of ITF inspectors in ports worldwide. The ITF's agreements with employers are distinctive in that they reflect a serious and prolonged industrial campaign, but also in three further ways. First, they have required that affiliates at least share bargaining with the GUF. Second, these agreements cover wages. Third, they are policed by a co-ordinated ITF inspectors' network, supported by regular educational activities allowing them to meet, develop contacts and exchange experience.

Koch-Baumgarten has cogently argued that there were three circumstances that brought this unique situation about. Firstly, the FOC nations were located in the developing world and were at the time of the campaign's origins essentially union-free, allowing the transfer of collective bargaining responsibilities from national level to the ITF. Secondly, the unions in labour-exporting countries were not to be influential in ITF decision-taking processes for some time to come, allowing the capital-exporting countries to enforce and consolidate the system. Finally, port union controls could be used to discipline potential conflict, both between unions and between unions and the FOC employers. The ITF was gradually able to build the commitment of unions from all countries to the campaign (Lillie, 2004). Nevertheless, the campaign arose, as Koch-Baumgarten shows, from a very specific set of historical circumstances unlikely to be replicated.

It is anticipated within the internationals that IFAs can also be extended to sectoral employers' associations where these exist at international level. Sectoral agreements are clearly easier, and cheaper, for GUFs to make than agreements with large numbers of individual employers. Whether employers who are tending to move away from national level employers' associations will be inclined to move towards them at international level is, however, unclear (Croucher et al., 2006).

As outlined above, IFAs normally include the eight ILO Core Labour Conventions: the freedoms of association and collective bargaining (87 and 98), against discrimination (100 and 111), forced labour (29, 105) and child labour (138, 182). An important right contained in the Danone agreement but absent from many others is that contained in C.135, 'rights of workers' representatives in the undertaking'. Other labour standards could in theory be included, such as those enshrining the right to strike, security of employment, access to decision makers and those regarding migrant workers. However, the conventions mentioned are generally restricted to the eight stated above. An ILO survey of those agreements signed before the end of July 2003 showed that 20 per cent did not even include Conventions 87 and 98, while mentions of other conventions were even fewer (ILO, 2003). Some, such as the Volkswagen agreement, make only indirect reference to the Core Labour Standards.

The IUF has developed a way of dealing with the current weak focus on union recognition in the agreements, designed to educate both affiliates and companies more fully on their purpose. It has signed a number of national and international Labour Recognition Agreements with multinationals, whose limited but clear aim is to secure union organising and bargaining rights. These agreements emphasise arguably the most important rights covered by an IFA and, because of their relatively sharp focus, may be a more effective way of helping unions build their organising and bargaining capacity. Increasingly, GUFs are trying at review meetings with companies to formulate and agree clearer and more specific language in IFAs, particularly on the right to organise. The IUF's move towards highlighting the organising and bargaining rights issue is clearly a departure of fundamental importance for the whole international union movement. It brings the vital question of local union rights much more clearly into focus.

Hammer (2005) suggests that one effect of IFAs is to extend company level agreements up supply chains to suppliers. In general, however, multinationals resist strong clauses mentioning suppliers. In fact, in some agreements such clauses do not exist (Schömann et al., 2008). With few exceptions, when these clauses appear, they simply specify that companies should 'inform' and 'encourage' their immediate suppliers, ignoring the extended supply chain, and there is no hint of sanctions if they do not conform (Schömann et al., 2008). The Lafarge agreement reproduced in Annex 2 says 'Lafarge will seek to use the services of those trading partners, subcontractors and suppliers which observe the principles agreed'. The Prym–IMF–European Works Council agreement simply 'encourages and supports their business partners to consider this declaration in their own respective company policy [sic]'. Even the proposed clauses in the IMF model agreement are not strong: 'X company supports and encourages its suppliers to take into account these principles in their own corporate policy.'

The IMF obviously regards a more stringent model clause as unrealistic. The Lukoil agreement arguably has a stronger but essentially similar version of this type of clause:

The Agreement covers all activities and operations where Lukoil has direct control. Where Lukoil does not have overall control it will exercise its best efforts in order to secure compliance with the standards and principles set out in the Agreement. Lukoil will notify its contractors, licensees and major suppliers of the existence of the Agreement and encourage them to comply with the standards and principles contained within it.

Lukoil–ICEM–ROGWU Agreement 2004

The absence or weak wording of these clauses is significant in the context of widespread externalisation and the fact that the great majority of workers are not directly employed by multinationals. This weakness primarily reflects company resistance to including more substantive terms and conditions.

Implementing and Managing Agreements

The implementation and management of these agreements is a critical area. Local management, like some local unions, are often neither aware of, nor committed to, an agreement signed by senior management in Western Europe. Unions can remedy this situation by reporting problems through agreements' review processes. Local company management can be surprised to learn that these processes exist. In Asia and Latin America, national union federations are weak and incapable of providing much assistance, so management in local operations generally do not anticipate that unions can muster any level of technical or political support. However, the actual incidence of this sort of reporting does not appear to be high.

There is little evidence that local unions have exploited these agreements. The BWI (2004) evaluation suggested that 'currently only a handful of unions are active in using the framework agreements and many are unaware of their purpose or even of their existence'. Vic Thorpe and Celia Mather, highly experienced international trade unionists reporting on the ITGLWF's project designed to conclude IFAs, wrote that 'Many affiliates interviewed had no clear idea of the nature or purpose of an International Framework Agreement' (2005: 7). It is worth noting that this ignorance was despite the project's specific efforts to inform them. Thorpe and Mather went on to recommend a more 'up from below' approach to generate more support (Thorpe and Mather, 2005: 7–8). Such an 'up from below' approach could include involving affiliates more fully in implementation and review processes than at present.

There are currently two approaches to monitoring both IFAs and unilateral company codes. A model promoted by BWI and ITGLWF is of direct GUF supervision and systematic monitoring of suppliers. BWI argues that establishing monitoring groups as part of an IFA's terms is an important tool for monitoring and building the agreements, particularly in companies with long sub-contracting and supply chains. The best-documented example comes from the favourable Scandinavian context. The BWI–IKEA agreement established an IKEA Monitoring Group, made up of BWI, IKEA and Swedish trade union representatives aimed at developing good industrial relations. Joint missions were carried out by the Monitoring Group in response to complaints from Slovakia, Hungary, Malaysia, Romania, Poland, Thailand, Laos and China. IKEA then set up a Compliance and Monitoring Group to manage IKEA's own code for suppliers. According to the company, this structure carried out training for 80 IKEA auditors and it is claimed that between 2000 and 2003 twenty thousand corrective actions were carried out as a result of audits. The model is essentially one of joint policing from headquarters, thereby at one level overcoming the issue of weak and uneven union representation in many of the company's workplaces outside of Sweden. It satisfies the company's requirement for reduction of labour-related CSR risk and clearly brings benefits to workers. The clear danger for the global union, however, is that the process plays too small a role in building trade unionism outside of the headquarter country.

The second model, used by IUF, UNI, IMF and ICEM, is more collaborative (Fichter and Sydow, 2002) and designed to build affiliates' capacity to monitor and use complaints and review mechanisms. This model is closely tied to the formation of company networks that potentially facilitate complaints being raised. Recently, a method of monitoring has been agreed at Peugeot–Citroen that envisages more decentralised processes. The agreement will be monitored by 'social observatories' to be established at local level involving management and unions according to terms of reference to be agreed by the local parties. The involvement of local unions provides a direct voice for them that would otherwise be absent, and they are clearly more involved in this case than in most. Such an arrangement promotes confidence that local representatives will understand the agreement's content and how it should be applied.

To offer real possibilities for unions outside of Europe to organise, IFAs need to clearly state practical, concrete and specific rights at the workplace. That is, they must be capable of being used by local unions and not simply vague statements by companies of general responsibilities. In this respect, the IUF approach of making them recognition agreements has a good deal to offer.

Conclusion

What impact might IFAs have on building local capacity to bargain and organise? It is important to answer this question within a global perspective, since only a tiny minority of the world's workers are employed in these companies. This is unlikely to change rapidly, and if the internationals cannot organise workers well beyond multinationals their legitimacy as representatives of global labour is likely to be threatened.

Although IFAs set frameworks, the way this is done means that their impact may always be minimal. Limits exist for further developing agreements through review processes if the current balance of forces between local unionists and managements in the developing world – where the latter possess an overwhelming advantage – remains or, as seems more likely, worsens. The building workers' evaluation of these agreements reached a similar conclusion:

> There is an urgent need for more and better involvement of affiliated trade unions and for them to take greater responsibilities. This will require a training programme to assist unions to take up the challenge of recruiting and organising in those companies.

> (BWI, 2004)

It seems more important to help trade unionists to operate both technically and politically within multinationals than to attempt to create agreements they cannot use. As Ingeborg Wick concludes in relation to her research on IFAs and unilateral codes of practice, there is a need to strengthen union capacities to take advantage of them, 'particularly in the developing world' (Wick, 2004: 127). This can be seen as part of the wider process of explaining and promoting international régimes that was identified many years ago as important to any such régime's diffusion and survival (Olson, 1965). Developing networks of trade unionists at both company and regional levels can potentially play a part in this, and this is the subject of our next chapter.

CHAPTER SIX

Networks

Introduction

INTERNATIONAL networks of trade unionists are clearly useful for unions attempting to make IFAs into meaningful organising tools. Moreover, because they help to build unions' engagement with other unions internationally, they are key to delivering international solidarity action.

Defining 'networks' is problematic as the term is used by GUFs in multiple and often confusing ways – sometimes to describe *ad hoc* groupings, sometimes committees and even to describe a GUF (Union Network International). By 'network' here we mean stable groups of union representatives from different units of a multinational company or sector who are in communication with each other. A degree of stability and permanence is required for the description to be meaningful, as in many cases networks have been formally established but have no continuing existence (Greven, 2006). Finally, networks should be identifiable as such within the trade unions and membership should be possible. In practice, networks take quite different forms, with differing levels of involvement of works councils, headquarters and non-headquarters unions, management and GUFs. From a union viewpoint, networks' aims vary and may develop across time, but they are generally set up initially to collect and exchange information with the aim of progressing towards organising, coordination and solidarity action.

Company networks are of strategic significance to GUFs (Garver et al., 2007). The IMF World Auto Council identified both IFAs and 'timely, accurate and accessible information' through networks as central, related tasks for the IMF in 2004 (IMF, 2004). The BWI evaluation of IFAs similarly suggested that to succeed, they would require 'substantially improved communication and global networking' (BWI, 2004).

The central argument of this chapter is that the networks in existence are in these terms problematic. Staggeringly, given their strategic importance and the substantial GUF resources dedicated to them, there are no examples of truly global company networks. There are no networks with global scope that relate directly to existing International Framework Agreements. This is largely because of pockets of non-unionism, non-affiliation by some unions and because many companies take pains to keep agreements and networks apart. However, important methodological and procedural problems also hamper network development.

To be described as successful, a network should deliver demonstrable benefits to workers. In this chapter, five key factors are identified that underlie successful networks: how they are formed, company attitudes and influence, resources, the network's ability to facilitate participation of diverse memberships, and the spatial basis of that membership. Existing company networks show that self-interest and a potential increase in bargaining power with employers are insufficient to generate the high level of engagement required to achieve success. The networks that we examine which function at higher levels exhibit 'significant commonality' (Olmsted, 1959: 21) and encourage a depth of engagement that goes beyond the instrumental. The network members are aware of having something significant in common; that is, a commitment to *international* trade unionism.

The chapter concludes with the suggestion that the best way to develop sufficient commitment from network members is to build engagement by working in small groups, or 'minilaterally' as defined in Chapter three, using participatory educational tools.

A Functioning Regional Network

That networks have great potential for unions is exemplified by the ICEM's Caspian Energy Network, formally established in 2005 in a region and sector of major strategic importance to the GUF. The Caspian Sea region, with the world's third largest oil and gas reserves behind the Middle East and Russia is likely to become a major energy exporter over the next decade. Currently, these countries are relatively minor producers due to specific political, economic and technical factors. Major multinational oil and gas companies operate in Azerbaijan, the centre of oil production in the region, through a consortium. BP, Chevron, ENI-Agip and Lukoil are involved and the Norwegian oil company Statoil is a small but significant consortium member. The Azeri state oil company Socar is a major player in exploration and development, directly employing around seventy thousand people. Numerous new pipeline projects have been proposed. Some are under construction, the most significant being the Caspian Pipeline Consortium Project, the Baku–Tiblisi–Ceyhan oil pipeline and the South Caucasus natural gas pipeline Baku–Tiblisi–Ersurum. These and other projects involve countries outside the Caspian region, notably Turkey, Georgia, Iran and the countries of Central Asia.

The oil unions in the former Soviet Union were until the early twenty-first century entirely enclosed in bureaucratic relations with their state employers, with no experience of or, in many cases, interest in organising workers in the growing number of private companies. Long-term contact between the leaderships of the Norwegian, Russian and Azeri unions led to discussion of forging a strategic alliance and opened the Azeri union to wider perspectives. These unions represented the most significant groups of union membership and concentrations of available resources, particularly in relation to access to company management. For more than five years the unions, in partnership with the ICEM, engaged in educational work and associated relationship building, developing strong communication links between future network members. Thus, the group's evolution allowed time for educational processes to occur.

At the initial network meeting, union participation was as broad as possible, given that there were no contacts in Iran and Turkmenistan and only weak links with Kazak ICEM affiliates. The meeting was held on the basis that participants would be free to set up the kind of network they thought would be effective. Group participation was high, allowing unions to set group goals highly congruent with individual interests and to form an informed, realistic view of what could be achieved. Active learning methods were used, and focussed aims established through in-depth discussion about the network's purpose. These aims included the identification of business and trade union partners willing to enter into dialogue, and the development of negotiation skills in union representatives. Significantly, the network also decided on immediate tasks, including research, negotiation and organising activities. The process allowed the core group of Azeri, Russian and Norwegian unions to persuade less-engaged members to increase their commitment. Both the strategic and immediate targets were concrete and achievable but group aims were set to the highest, rather than the lowest, common denominator. The network agreed collectively to attend an international oil sector conference taking place in Baku the following year in order to find possible company targets and present the network publicly.

During the visit to Baku the network directly assisted the Azeri Oil and Gas Workers' Union (OGWU), which until this point exclusively organised permanent workers in the state oil company Socar, to organise private sector employees. The union had only limited experience of organising and none of managing strike action. In November 2005 two thousand workers employed by Socar, BP and the American-based contractor McDermott, supported by OGWU, went on strike for union recognition, medical care, improved pay and contracts. The Caspian Energy Network members, all senior leaders in their own countries, assisted OGWU's President, Jahangir Aliyev, to manage the negotiations and to carry out a recruitment campaign to organise private sector workers. The network used the national media to pressure the employers' consortium, highlighting the issues involved and announcing the presence of union leaderships from across the region, supported internationally by the ICEM.

OGWU organised 5,000 private sector workers during this campaign. Shortly afterwards, 1,600 workers employed at the offshore BosShelf site, a French–Azeri construction project partially owned by Bouygues, joined OGWU following a strike. Union negotiations brought improvements for workers. Several of the companies now recognise Azerbaijan's national celebratory days and official holidays. These strikes proved to be historic breakthroughs in the Baku area, because a wave of similar actions followed. At the time of writing, workers in another fourteen companies have been engaged in industrial action also bringing improvements to contract workers' terms and conditions. Most recently, in June 2008 OGWU negotiated increases of more than 100 per cent in minimum salaries and obtained health and safety improvements for over one thousand contract workers at Caspian Shipyards.

The network was therefore able to perform a high level of 'locomotion' (Olmsted, 1959: 113), or mobilisation, based on the high level of cohesiveness built within the primary group. This cohesiveness was, in turn, based on the high capacity of network members to communicate, developed through the educational approach to relationship building. The wave of organising and negotiating successes in Baku galvanised the network, providing a precedent for organising in the private sector that showed results which members in other countries promoted in their own unions. Several other unions in the network are now moving beyond their enclosed state oil company horizons to organise more widely.

Company and Sectoral Networks

The Caspian Energy Network contextualises our analysis of company and sectoral networks because many are less evidently successful in delivering benefits to workers. There is in fact little reliable information about the numbers and workings of the networks supported by different GUFs, reflecting the latters' nervousness that a gap exists between theory and practice in this area. The number of genuine networks operating in each GUF is likely to be in single figures.

In what follows, the five key factors in developing networks mentioned above are highlighted and illustrated from the limited evidence available.

The first factor to consider is how networks are formed. The Caspian Energy Network was created after a long process of relationship building. The core unions at the network's centre had brought their relations to the point at which they were already strongly committed to the idea of a regional network before the founding meeting. At the meeting, network aims were developed from the bottom up and attracted the broadest possible participation. This contrasts sharply with the normal process whereby a GUF or union raises money for a meeting, and then invites unions to join a 'global network'. There are normally short preparation periods for these meetings and the scope of the proposed organisation is already set from outside. In addition, relationships are generally too weak to build commitment and a focus on practical issues is lacking. Expectations are raised beyond what is achievable, particularly in view of the actual resources available, which are seen as almost exclusively the GUF's responsibility to acquire. The network is then in practice frequently reduced to a small 'global steering committee' with little wider involvement.

Although the few existing accounts pay little attention to them, company attitudes and influence are another key factor. Since resources are a major issue, in almost all cases management plays a role in providing the conditions for networks to exist. Frequently, network meetings divide their time between union-only pre- and post-meetings, as well as joint meetings with management. Management structures often conceptualise them as 'employee consultative councils', similar to national level or European Works Councils but without the same legal basis. Companies are anxious, as Schömann et al. (2008: 46) point out, to avoid trade union organisations 'becoming real negotiating partners on working conditions' at international level. Thus, for example, Unilever expressed its preference for company-based forms of representation such as works councils over trade unions to Schömann and her colleagues. In common with many management structures, they prefer to avoid the 'outside influence' of unions, and to build close relationships with in-company representatives. However, these can be too close. The Volkswagen World Works Council (VWWC) appears to have the strongest structure and most cooperative relationship with management. But it has also become clear that the nature of the relationships between company and works council in the national level German codetermination bodies that form the basis for the VWWC went well beyond cooperation. Their corruption amounted to a major public scandal that still threatens to discredit the entire system of codetermination in Germany.

As we remarked above, a disjuncture exists between IFAs and company networks. In the cases of the signed IFAs listed in Table 9 in Chapter five there appear to be only a few functioning regional and no global networks corresponding to them. The explanation, it has been suggested to us, is simple: managements do not wish the two to coexist and, given their role in allowing paid time off and funding travel and accommodation for those who attend, they often have the power to make sure that they do not.

A common theme of the limited discussion that has taken place on this subject by others is that structural and process difficulties may be overcome, but only if more resources become available (Müller and Rüb, 2005; Miller, 2004). That is, the cost of running networks poses a serious challenge to already stretched union finances. A 'global network' meeting costs between thirty thousand and seventy-five thousand Euros and approximately three quarters of the network's potential membership is likely to lack the resources to pay for their participation. Since global networks are seen as the responsibility of the coordinating GUF, it is assumed that they must either raise project funding from donors or from companies themselves. A second possible resourcing strategy is for the headquarters union to carry the main burden of administration and activity costs. This inevitably tends to further increase the weight of that union within the network. Networking underlines the resource crisis facing the internationals. Either unions at national level will have to commit more resources to international work, or networking will remain inadequate to the tasks.

The fourth factor to consider is the network's ability to facilitate the participation of diverse memberships. This is affected by the complexity of communication within international networks (Miller et al., 2000). Communication at international level is difficult, for both practical and political reasons. In many countries, and probably the majority, union activists have only limited English or second language capacity. In most developing countries activist access to computers is extremely limited and telecommunications are often unreliable for providing timely responses to other network members' messages. Even when the practicalities of communication are somehow managed, most activists from the developing world are entering an entirely unfamiliar forum in a 'global' network. At network meetings members must explicitly state their own interests, understand those of other unions and critically assess the network's potential. This all has to be done within a relatively short period of two to three days, often with little pre-meeting information or previous contact with other network members. Groups of diverse and often inexperienced participants find it difficult to successfully navigate such situations.

Levels of union organisation in multinationals are uneven. This can limit the scope of network membership, with totally unorganised sites and others with low density coexisting with well organised ones. These disparities create a situation of unequal weight and influence between units which has to be managed to ensure that genuine collaboration becomes possible. The more truly international the network is, the greater are the socio-economic differences that must be confronted. As discussed in previous chapters, considerable differences exist between the politics and approaches of unions from different traditions, to the extent that cohesion can become almost impossible to achieve.

None of this is to deny that interests can be aggregated, but the difficulties in developing full participation are considerable. Clearly, the internal dynamics of the network count, in particular whether the network helps members from developing regions genuinely to participate.

The problems are graphically illustrated through the example of an international network within the US tyre manufacturer Goodyear. The United Steel Workers of America (USWA) funded the initiation of the Goodyear Global Union Network in March 1999, at an event attended by over one hundred trade unionists from sixteen countries. In 2006 the USWA started the Goodyear Newsletter, during a strike against Goodyear in the US and Canada, called 'Global Solidarity'. By the account provided by a representative of the Thai workers involved, the network later proved incapable of defending a victimised activist.

In 2005 Anan Pol-ung, President of the Thai Goodyear union PCFT was sacked for trying to negotiate improved benefits and permanent contracts for twenty-five contract workers on annual contracts. In October 2005 all of these workers were sacked, and all direct employment of contract workers by Goodyear was terminated. Goodyear then used external labour agencies to employ workers in these functions. Anan was simultaneously reinstated, although at a lower grade.

The Thai Industrial Relations Court ruled for the reinstatement of the contract workers in April 2006. When the remaining sixteen workers (two had died in the intervening period) appeared at the factory for work in May 2006, management refused them entry. In August 2006 Anan was sacked for a second time for failing to attend a meeting because he had to attend to his comatose mother in hospital.

The ICEM was contacted by the Thai union PCFT requesting solidarity support. The ICEM ensured that the dispute was understood and recorded, and contacted the United Steelworkers of America. The GUF built a high-profile information and solidarity campaign, as this represented one of the first attempts by a small local union to organise and bargain for contract workers, a priority issue. After repeated requests, the United Steel Workers of America agreed to invite Anan Pol-ung to discuss the case during the two-day Global Goodyear Unions' Network Meeting in Akron, Ohio, USA 19–20 March 2007. The meeting was attended by ICEM representatives and its most powerful affiliates, including the South African NUM and the German IG BCE. Despite this representation, when Anan's case was raised in the meeting with management, the Goodyear HR representative was allowed simply to comment that he tried not to be involved in matters outside the US and that he would refer the case to the manager in charge of Thailand. The outcome is regarded by the Thai workers as a network failure, particularly since they had managed to overcome major barriers in bringing the case to international attention. Despite heavy backing by the GUF, the Thai activists did not obtain even moral support from the network, including from the developed country trade unionists present.

International company networks are too frequently dominated by headquarters unions, leaving no space for weaker and smaller unions to genuinely participate in network development and work. Several longstanding networks have made little or no progress in addressing this major problem. The Daimler–Chrysler World Employee Committee, formed after the merger between the two companies as an extension of German works council arrangements, provides an example. Some unions outside of the key Europe–North America company axis are not involved, while the IMF has only an advisory role. In the view of both of these unions and the IMF, the network pays too little attention to the need to construct and aid organisation in the developing world.

A second example is that of the Nestlé network, whose development is shown in Table 10. This network's origins are tied up with significant international action, in which the right of a Peruvian union to operate was successfully defended, via the IUF and a New Zealand affiliate (Rütters, 2001). This initial impetus was important to all concerned, but, predictably, proved hard to maintain.

Table 10: The Nestlé Network

Phase	Objectives	Participants	Activities	Funding
1972–1979	Networking & information exchange, planning/feasibility	Global	2 IUF conferences, informal contact with Nestlé management	IUF/Affiliates' own expense
1980s	Networking & information exchange	EU, North America	2 regional networking events	Affiliates' own expense, Nestlé European Council
1993–1999	Development of 3 regional networks, global networking and information exchange, establishment of network objectives	Africa, Latin America, Asia-Pacific	1 global & 3 regional meetings, Manila Declaration	LO Norway
2002–2004	Coordinated information exchange, networking and campaigning	Africa, Latin America, Eastern Europe, Asia-Pacific	4 regional & 1 global meeting	FES, NGG, IUF
2004–2007	Coordination of information and networking in 4 regions	Africa, Latin America, Eastern Europe, Asia-Pacific	4 half-time coordinators	FES

Source: Levinson (1972) and Rüb (2004)

The IUF report on the Nestlé network (Rüb, 2004), as it has functioned more recently, raises structural and process issues about the way that internal dialogue is conducted. Agendas and procedural matters are used to deal formally with issues that are of interest mainly to headquarters unions, and there are too few possibilities for delegates to address problems outside of this framework.

The key to successful aggregation of interests between representatives of workplaces with different interests from unions of very different types and of facilitating the necessary learning process is, Hoffmann (2005) suggested, a discursive and transparent way of operating that acknowledges differences of interests and tries openly to find common ground. This underlines the relevance of using educational methods, which assist networks in developing open and participative approaches, as Erne (2006; 2008) has shown. Doug Miller, an experienced worker educator with the ITGLWF, provides guidance on appropriate processes (Miller, 2004). His sensitive analysis is especially useful precisely because it derives from a sector with relatively weak union organisation, which tends to magnify the problems associated with network building. The methods Miller advocates are: a multi-level research effort by unions on the company, awareness raising to build networks, a flexible approach by the GUF, and coordinated campaigns with other interested organisations such as NGOs (an approach that is especially relevant to the weakly organised ITGLWF). Thus part of his prescription is similar to ours since he advocates an inclusive, flexible approach facilitated by strong research and two-way educational processes broadly defined.

The fifth and final factor that influences network functionality is the spatial basis for membership. The network operating in the German chemical multinational BASF illustrates the point, because there is no central dialogue, but rather a set of regional networks established over a period of around ten years. This is a highly devolved structure, sustained by a combination of external project funding from the Friedrich Ebert Stiftung and company finance, and built on a regional basis with involvement from the ICEM. It is viewed within the GUF as relatively successful since regional dialogue with management has been secured in Latin America and Asia. Coordinated bargaining within each region has been achieved, albeit to different extents. The right to organise has also been won in practice, most notably in some Latin American workplaces. Definite gains have therefore been made, although how much this has been brought about by the network is harder to ascertain. The BASF example indicates the significance of the degree of devolution of the networks' structures and power relations. It is an example of the benefits of working within smaller groups, in this case with a smaller geographic scope. The problem of language is to some degree alleviated by working within sub-regional or regional groups. Although this will have a limited effect in the Asia region, it impacts much more in Latin America and the former Soviet Union.

We summarise our interpretations of the five networks discussed above in Table 11 below. We note the limited level of solidarity action, mobilisation and bargaining success that the networks have managed to achieve, despite many years of activity. All of the networks discussed claim some success, but their achievements, although real, are so far limited to a few documented instances. Some limited space has been created for trade unionists outside of the developed world. The Daimler–Chrysler network succeeded in successfully raising the right of Turkish workers at the Ditas plant to organise, and has dealt with other complaints raised through its consultative structure with management. In Nestlé, the network's origins were linked to successful international solidarity action. Later, it was able to provide moral support to an important strike at a plant in Korea, with the union consolidating its position and membership through public action and the network in turn gaining impetus through that.

The most substantial, if uneven, bargaining successes appear to have been achieved by the BASF regional networks. The regional Caspian Sea network has also delivered considerable gains to workers.

Table 11: Interpretive Summary of Five Networks

Company/ Sector	Initiator	Motives	Achievements	Disadvantages
Caspian Energy Project	ICEM NOPEF ROGWU OGWU	Build bargaining & organising capacity in the Caspian	Organising private sector workers Establishing regional network	Requires high level of GUF and union staff resources No real capacity to include organisations from Turkmenistan and Iran
Goodyear	USWA	Establish global information and campaigning network to support national negotiations	Information exchange	No capacity for direct solidarity action
Nestlé	IUF	Inability to secure dialogue with Nestlé management	Information exchange Solidarity mechanism High-profile IUF activity	No dialogue at national, regional or international levels Unsustainable financially
DaimlerChrysler	IG Metall German Works Council	Secure information and coordination between key plants Ensure IG Metall control of international dialogue	Resolution of several disputes	No real IMF role No real developing country influence Weak agreement with company Unable to sustain commitment of unions globally
BASF	IG BCE ICEM GWC	Establish regional social dialogue outside Western Europe	Regional dialogue in Latin America and Asia Networking contacts in Eastern Europe	No IFA No global dialogue; failure to engage North American management and unions

Conclusion

The conclusions here mesh with arguments made elsewhere in the book that working within small groups and with an educational focus offers an immediately viable way of networking. Five key factors have been identified as important to networking success: how networks are formed, company attitudes and influence, resources, the potential for participation and the spatial basis of membership. In terms of how networks are formed, time and resources are clearly needed for the educational processes required. Company attitudes and influence are closely linked to the resources issue; networks' degree of independence needs to be as high as possible and therefore more independent funding is needed. At present, IFAs and networks are being kept apart by companies who dispose of the necessary resources.

Maximising membership participation in the network is largely determined by whether the power dynamics between unions from developed (particularly the headquarters unions) and developing countries can be managed successfully. The use of an educational approach helps this to be managed effectively; what this entails is explored in the next chapter. How networks are run is a major issue and taking an educational approach to networking raises the potential for generating the other success factors. Education allows network members to communicate their own interests and relate to those of others in ways that build psychological engagement. Importantly, it strengthens the link between membership identification with the network and their behaviour. A network's capacity to mobilise union activity and resources is also increased because targets are well understood and articulated. This level of engagement is fundamental to building a strong communication foundation.

The most successful examples of high levels of engagement involve small groups of unions, normally brought together on a regional or sub-regional basis. These small, closely related groups are able to achieve higher degrees of mutual understanding, cohesion and coordinated action than existing networks. The point about the effectiveness of regional as opposed to global networking already appears well taken in some GUFs. Thus, the IMF's World Auto Council has argued to the IMF that improved regional structures should underpin their World Auto Councils (IMF, 2004).

This discussion has implications for the question raised in the previous chapter regarding how to proceed with IFAs. Following the analysis laid out in this chapter it is clear networks that still need to be built effectively to use IFAs should, from their inception, be created on a minilateral or regional basis, with the bulk of resources devoted to educational activities rather than, as at present, to global steering committee meetings. This is an essential reorientation.

CHAPTER SEVEN

International Union Education

It is important to realise that this tool for the union, education, keeps on being improved and used to keep the movement going forward. In general, trade union education is an essential tool for the unions as it has the capacity to allow them to define where they are, where they want to be and how they will get to where they want to be. It is a tool for unions to deal with the challenges of today's globalised workplace and the MNC.

(The African trade unionist who provided this
quotation has asked to remain anonymous.)

Education helps to build solidarity between workers at local, national and international level. Through affiliation with ITF and participation in ITF education courses, our airline union learned and had information exchanges with similar unions in other countries. In one airline company, many protest letters were sent to management in Thailand and they were forced to improve the work rules.

Aranya Pakapath, ICEM Project Coordinator Thailand

Introduction

THIS chapter examines trade union education in the international context. We refer here to educational work carried out primarily by the internationals, which although it is often linked to that carried out at national level, is distinctive because of the involvement of trade unionists from more than a single country. Trade union education has historically been, and remains, a central tool of the internationals' work and this is unsurprising since some major national unions had their origins in educational activity. In most GUFs funding spent on this area is equivalent to income from affiliation fees and consumes more staff resources than any other area of work, even though its full import and significance are not always grasped.

Our argument here has four related strands. First, education broadly conceived is indispensable for helping unions to socialise activists, arm them with arguments and confidence to tackle their problems, form networks and develop their organisations. Second, the union educational model, which emphasises egalitarian, transparent and discursive approaches to defining and solving problems, is ideally suited to international activities. Third, the world's unions are extremely diverse and have a wealth of experience in dealing with workers' problems. This very diversity, often referred to as a major problem in international unionism, can be turned to advantage through positive use. Exchanges of experience and the results of experimentation can be shared constructively in educational environments. Finally, and crucially for both unions and the internationals themselves, education strongly stimulates democratic involvement. It has been shown that unions can become 'learning democracies' whereby the informal processes of collective learning coexist with, supplement and support more formal representative democracy (Huzzard, 2000).

International Union Education: Definitions, Extent, Significance and Methods

We adopt a broad definition of education. We include within it all forms of activity designed to build unions' capacities to deal with members' problems, from formal programmes of education at one end of the spectrum to secondments, informal consultancy and coaching at the other. Nevertheless, the primary activity we are referring to consists of classroom-based programmes of structured discussion and participant-centred activities. These approaches can also be used to good effect outside of classrooms, and supplemented by the other methods we refer to.

The number of trade unionists participating in education at any one point is extremely difficult to estimate with any degree of accuracy because basic data are unavailable. Nevertheless, we attempt a very broad estimate here since it is important to have some idea of its global reach.

It is likely that on average a GUF works with approximately fifty unions from developing countries each year and educates somewhere between five hundred and five thousand unionists at grassroots and leadership levels, i.e. between ten and one hundred per union. Therefore if the number of union participants lies somewhere between these poles of ten and one hundred, then the global total is in the region of around 25,000 a year for all GUFs. This is a relatively small proportion of total membership, since the membership of ITUC affiliates is around 167 million. Nevertheless, over the last twenty-five years of global union programmes, hundreds of thousands of trade unionists are likely to have received some level of education. A large percentage of these participants have maintained their activism and some have taken senior positions. A good deal of scope remains for further development, because some of these participants are likely only to have had brief contact with union education.

Some further insight into the proportion of members involved can be gleaned from rough estimates of the numbers touched by the relatively large educational effort made by the internationals and others in the former Soviet Union. An external evaluation of international union educational work there admitted that figures are difficult to give with confidence. This comprehensive report, produced by a team of researchers led by Irina Khaliy of the Russian Academy of Sciences (2005), estimated that the total number of people involved over the ten years between 1994 and 2004 exceeded 300,000. The total formal membership of the Russian unions alone in 2004 was around 34 million; therefore around one member in one thousand had experienced some involvement. Recognising that the aim was to train the vital activist layer rather than all members, the report suggested that the extent of the work was 'truly significant' but that much remained to be done to increase the numbers involved: 'There are still thousands of willing activists at workplace level who need practical assistance to help them in the new functions they know they must perform' (Khaliy, 2005: 3). Thus, even here, where major efforts have been made, many remain untouched. Sogge (2004) pointed out that despite the upsurge in international bodies' efforts in the former Soviet Union, many requests for assistance could not be met.

The internationals are responsible for coordinating the educational effort. They are well placed to carry out, commission, supervise and expand educational work since they have unique expertise in international industrial relations. They are living concentrations of accumulated historical knowledge, a profound asset from which affiliates and their activists stand to benefit. They also have many experienced individuals who can be described as 'bridge builders', people who have been identified as being important in helping trade unionists from different backgrounds to work together in effective ways (Garver et al., 2007). The internationals' staff are aware of best practice in union educational methods although they are often less aware of the applicability of these methods outside of the classroom situation in, for example, network-building contexts. As we argued in the previous chapter, this is an issue that needs attention.

We show the typical aims, subjects, forms and results of trade union education in international contexts in Table 12 below. Union education has an overarching aim, i.e. one that applies to all of its forms: to raise trade unionists' and workers' confidence in their capacity to tackle their own problems collectively. Underneath this umbrella aim, a good number of secondary aims have also existed.

The first and perhaps most obvious is to develop unions' capacity to carry out representative functions on behalf of their members, both directly by improving representational capacity and indirectly by addressing union structures, management and ways of working. Many unions worldwide do not have extensive experience of representation nor of organising or mobilising workers. In the case of unions from the ex-Communist countries for example, education has recently meant demonstrating the relevance of unions adopting organising, mobilising and representational

Table 12: Typical Target Groups, Subjects, Aims, Forms and Results of International Trade Union Education

Target Group and Subject	Aims	Forms	Results
Union officers and workplace representatives: representing workers (Typical topics: organising and mobilising workers, health and safety, negotiating)	Improve worker representation	Formal education programmes, study circles	Improved worker representation, democratising effects in unions
Union officers, representatives and workers: training for paralegal representatives	Provide free representation in legal contexts	Formal education programmes	Systems of free workers' representation in industrial courts, legal arbitration systems
Trade union tutors: 'training trainers'	Increase available pool of worker educators	Formal education programmes, 'micro-teaching', coaching and mentoring, information, materials exchange through newsletters etc.	Creation and maintenance of pool of worker educators
Union officers and workplace representatives: union management and organisational development	Improve union structures, ways of working; improve participation of women and ethnic minorities	Formal educational programmes, inter-union exchanges	Improvements in union effectiveness; increased participation of women and ethnic minorities
Workplace representatives and workers: very wide range of workplace-based subjects including HIV/ AIDS peer counselling	Very wide range Peer counselling for HIV/ AIDS aim is to train peer counsellors	Formal educational programmes, study circles	Raise identification with union; specific outcomes such as creating body of HIV/AIDS peer counsellors
Workers	Raise workers' participation in unions and in HIV/AIDS programmes, skills training etc.	Wide range of formal and informal forms	Raised worker participation in unions and HIV/AIDS programmes, improved worker skills etc.

approaches. Issues of union structure and democracy are addressed, especially by encouraging the participation of women and ethnic minorities in union affairs, often through women-only courses (Reufter and Rutters, 2002). The second aim, from a more institutional perspective, has been to offer a practical and effective route out of the isolation and stagnation experienced by many unions in developing countries and to provide a much needed impetus for their organisational development. Programmes therefore aim to impart a sense that they are part of a wider global movement. More recently, a third aim has appeared: to raise levels of workers' participation in activities such as HIV/AIDS or skills development programmes. This type of work is controversial in terms of how faithfully it reflects trade union aims and how far it is primarily driven by a wish to access funding. In Britain, it has been argued that government support for building a system of workplace union learning representatives has in fact brought unions little and represents little more than a channelling of trade unionism to state ends (McIlroy, 2008). At this point, therefore, it may be that the overarching aim is not present.

At the global level, the educational emphasis has shifted in recent decades. In an initial phase, from the 1980s to the mid 1990s, the main thrust was towards diffusing union educational methods and building cadre systems. Partly because of the experience of the Scandinavian donors, this was based on essentially self-organised and directed study circles. These were experientially based, problem centred, highly adaptable and, not least, sustainable. From the late 1990s onwards, a second phase began as international trade union education directly attempted to stimulate more fundamental change in unions. In many cases union policies, financial structures and internal democracy were putting a brake on educational efforts and, more importantly, on broader structural changes. Education designed to make unions more effective, often masked in the language of 'renewal' or 'modernisation' to make it more acceptable to affiliates who might be offended by the idea that their organisations required overhaul, was launched.

The methods of trade union education used in international work have also undergone a revolution in the last twenty years. For much of the twentieth century, the predominant method was formal lecturing by experts to relatively passive groups of participants. This coexisted with a minority strand, which emphasised the importance of an experientially based, problem-solving, highly participative approach whereby participants negotiated between themselves and with tutors the concrete problems for discussion. Union educational work has more recently built on this minority strand and has drawn on a set of compatible, overlapping philosophies eclectically fused by the tutors concerned. A more or less standard component has been the active learning methods first devised in German workers' education in the 1920s (Feidel-Mertz, 1964). The 1920s theorists grappled with the problem of how to build an educational practice appropriate to the thousands of workplace representatives elected in German unions under the post-First World

War works constitution law. Their solution was essentially to begin by inducting accounts of problems from participants, and then to approach the issues by using the experience of those present, and inducting external resources such as the law, rather than beginning by explaining legal details. This was the origin of the current orthodoxy. In addition, tutors sometimes drew on the work of other theorists such as the Brazilian pedagogue Paulo Freire and his book *The Pedagogy of the Oppressed* (1970) to stress the emancipatory and empowering nature of education and collective activity.

All of these approaches encourage participants to step aside from their personal educational background or position in the union to acquire the tools to address real issues in the workplace. Lecturing has given way to problem-solving of concrete issues brought to the group, defined and intensively discussed, *inter alia* through simulation exercises. In the last decade, these methods, often under titles such as 'the new educational methods', or 'the ILO approach' after several important projects carried out by that organisation, have rapidly gained ground and have begun to displace traditional methods.

Participative education methods have provided many unions outside of the developed world with the only sustainable way of conducting education. They require virtually no facilities, a vital consideration since funding residential training has been beyond most unions' means. Dedicated buildings or large budgets are not necessary, and the methods provide ways of working that can be used in workplaces and local offices. Simultaneously, they are resource expanding since they greatly increase the contribution that unpaid activists can make.

Union educational methods are frequently preferable to normal trade union decision-taking environments that provide far less participation opportunities and are governed by more formal rules. Their insistence on the equal right of all to participate and to share their experience is important in this connection. They model a highly participative mode of decision-taking that supplements and balances the necessary formal meetings based on organisational agendas. This is particularly relevant where significant cultural differences and power imbalances exist. The problem-solving educational focus is also usefully polyvalent in relation to the external world in that it is not linked to a specific subject. It therefore helps unions respond to collective problems in the workplace and external shocks to their structures whatever their nature.

Although perceived differently by different unions internationally, union educational methods constitute a way of working recognised by most unions in the world. They therefore constitute a shared frame of reference that can be useful in providing a basis for constructing international networks through which the diversity of union functions, structures and modus operandi can be turned into a positive resource on which participants draw (Croucher, 2004).

Donors, Projects and Funding

The great majority of international union education is carried out through projects, funded by a small group of donor organisations. Referred to as development cooperation programmes they are, in the main, funded by the Dutch/Nordic trade union bodies, established to administer funds from national affiliates and tax payers. The funds come mainly from government, and to a more limited extent in the case of FNV, from clauses in collectively bargained contracts negotiated with employers. An exception is the ITF's FOC Campaign, funded through the Seafarers' Fund, i.e. largely by employers. Another is the prominent example of employer funding for development work through the IUF's joint programmes in the tobacco and chocolate sectors, but these do not provide funds directly for union education. In the cases of Sweden and Finland, national unions are expected to contribute co-funding for projects funded through the donor organisations. The ITUC estimated that in 2000, US$10,380,522 was raised for the internationals' development cooperation programmes. Given the large scale funding not included in the secretariat accounts used to compile these figures, this estimate is conservative.

The key donors for large projects have long been the Dutch FNV Mondiaal, LO-TCO Sweden, LO-FTF Denmark, LO Norway and SASK Finland. LO-TCO has the largest annual budget, at an estimated 13 million Euro for 2006, closely followed by FNV with 11.9 million Euro, and SASK with an unconfirmed annual budget of approximately 3 million Euro. In addition, the German Friedrich Ebert Foundation (FES), a social democratic foundation using predominantly governmental funds, provides extensive funding for more localised projects. Active in just under one hundred countries worldwide, it makes a significant contribution in a decentralised way. FES has a dedicated programme for the GUFs with an annual budget of 10–15 million Euro per year.

These organisations award and administer funding in two ways. The first is multilateral, i.e. by channelling money to the internationals and international NGOs. The second is bilateral, where money is provided direct to local unions and NGOs. The pattern of funding is shifting, with donors increasingly opting to make funds available for bilateral projects, mainly in partnership with civil society organisations other than unions. For example, the Danish LO-FTF over the last five years has moved away from working with GUFs, and their current contribution to the internationals' work is tiny. Given the significance of project funding for covering the internationals' core costs which we noted in Chapter four, any reduction in the extent to which their risk is spread across donors must be a matter for concern.

Table 13 below provides estimates of the balance of donors' funds allocated to bilateral and multilateral development projects in 2004. The table shows high levels of bilateral funding when measured against the funders' rhetorical commitment to the internationals.

Table 13: Estimated Bilateral/Multilateral Allocation of Trade Union Development Funds 2004

Solidarity Support Organisation (donor)	Bilateral	Multilateral
LO-TCO (Sweden)	25%	75%
FNV (Netherlands)	70%	30%
SASK (Finland)	25%	75%
LO-FTF (Denmark)	75%	25%
LO (Norway)	80%	20%

Source: Minutes of the Nordic-Dutch & GUF Meeting, Tuesday 5 April 2005
(Document in authors' possession)

It is increasingly difficult for GUFs to raise educational funding, for three reasons. The first is the election of more right wing governments in the Netherlands and Nordic countries, entailing increasingly stringent administrative requirements on the funding organisations which we detail below. The second is donors' anxiety that funding will be used to compensate for the internationals' declining income from affiliates. The third is that the majority of donor officials are increasingly drawn from outside the trade union movement and simply do not understand union objectives or their ways of operating. Their instinctive inclination is to work with NGOs.

Significant attempts to find new sources of funding to sustain project work are therefore being made. The reduced global amounts available from some funders (notably the FNV), and the political sensitivities of company funding have led the internationals to look towards other national aid structures, such as the British government's Department for International Development, and foundations. There has been a great expansion in the GUFs' large-scale funding in certain areas such as HIV/AIDS, and GUFs with affiliates in industries such as mining and transport (for example the ICEM and ITF) have taken some of this up. This work is clearly relevant to members' interests, but the wider risk is that the search for project funds makes the internationals increasingly subject to funders' different, sometimes problematic and constantly shifting, priorities.

Results

There have been few systematic studies of the results of international trade union education. One of the most extensive and detailed is the Khaliy report on work in the former Soviet Union, based on in-depth research throughout most of the country's regions. This suggested that the results of international educational work in the FSU had been highly significant, and that this had been underestimated both by the projects themselves and by the few Western researchers who took any interest. Unlike Khaliy's research team, Western researchers did not venture into the regions, while project coordinators often moved on to the next project rather than research the results of the previous one. The Khaliy report argued that the 'results were precisely those that could have been expected: unions became more radical and democratic' (Khaliy, 2005: 37). Similar results were found by David Sogge (2004), investigating the work that FNV Mondiaal supported in Eastern Europe and the former Soviet Union: the union problem was 'being turned around' as the title of his report put it. Perhaps the most eloquent testimony is that of the Federation of European Employers, whose website says that the Soviet-style FNPR unions in the former Soviet Union are 'much reformed'.

The results are closely linked to the processes set in train by the methods. The overarching result of union education is normally improved confidence to deal with problems collectively (Charoenloet et al., 2004). Several authors have also pointed out that education raises social capital between participants, thereby strengthening the links between them, and may also effect shifts in identity that bring about stronger union identification (Feidel-Mertz, 1964; Huzzard, 2000; Kirton and Healy, 2004). In our case, the identifications are international and can help to facilitate network building and the internationals' solidarity work in supporting activists in difficulty.

Participative methods have had a considerable and visible democratising effect on both the internationals themselves and their affiliates, with course participants going on to play a wide range of roles in representative bodies. Gumbrell-McCormick (2001) has shown how the ITUC's drive to improve women's participation at the international level in the late twentieth century was effective, when combined with other political measures in changing both the ITUC and its national affiliates. Studies at national level have shown how women's perceptions of their identities and their identification with unions can be raised by women-only courses (Kirton and Healy, 2004). Broadly similar results have been reported for educational work in the USA directed at increasing ethnic minority activism (Margolies, 2008). The democratising effect referred to by these researchers has been shown to occur even as a result of courses with other aims (Croucher and Halstead, 1990; Caldwell, 1998; Croucher, 2004).

As we show in many of the cases elsewhere in this book, activism in many national contexts carries considerable dangers to those involved, sometimes including risking their lives. In Latin American countries, trade unionism is 'high risk' activism since the murder of activists is common (Loveman, 1998). Educational activity can play a major part in establishing the dense and diverse national and international networks of support that can help to sustain activists. Relationships established through education have operated to support trade unionists working in the increasingly repressive states of Belarus and Moldova, facilitated exchanges of organising and bargaining information between them and helped the internationals to deepen their understanding of the situations in these countries (Croucher, 2004). In the next chapter we document further examples drawn from Colombia.

Results are also evident in terms of union organisational development. Significant improvements in this direction were reported by the five GUFs project that focused on the modernisation of unions in Russia, Ukraine, Azerbaijan, Kyrgyzstan and Kazakhstan. Started in 2004 and completed in 2008, this involved education on facilitating organisational change, together with close consultancy support to union leadership. In many of the unions, the project achieved a combination of 'hard' (structural and financial) and 'soft' (ways of working and cultural) change, albeit in differential ways depending on the pre-project readiness of unions to benefit. In Central Asia, the results have been relatively modest, involving mainly the establishment of educational schemes in the GUFs' affiliates. In Ukraine and to a lesser extent Russia, unions have been stimulated to go a good deal further. While they too have increased their educational effort, several have also shifted the balance in the distribution of subscription income more towards their national structures, thereby allowing meaningful coordinated organising and mobilising strategies to begin to be developed. For the first time, unions in the Ukraine outside the mining sector (where the independent miners' union must constantly organise in the face of determined opposition from managements and the official union) have undertaken organising drives (Guliy, 2008).

The effects of participating in GUF-led education are summarised succinctly by Mare Anceva of the Union of Industry, Energy and Mining of Macedonia:

> The Trade Union of Industry, Energy and Mining of Macedonia – SIER – is a member of two GUFs: IMF (since 1995) and ICEM (since 1996). SIER is a small union in a small country. When considering all the benefits that come with membership, it becomes very valuable, particularly for small unions and marginal economies.
>
> We in SIER appreciated very much the education projects, which resulted in building up union capacities, awareness of current global trends and broadening views regarding the organization itself, methods of work, etc. Of course, we had to find our own ways in all that (no copy and paste is ever possible in this work), but the influence and the welfare that came out of being a member of the GUFs are indisputable. GUFs are, first of all, very good and reliable sources of information. That is of greatest importance in dealing with privatization and FDI. Just meeting other colleagues, both from transition and developed countries and having the chance to exchange opinions and experiences is of special value.
>
> To explain what I mean, the *Train-the-trainer* project with ICEM/IUF resulted in having the first trainers within the union (which further resulted in a substantial increase in the educational activities carried on). The *Modernization* project

resulted in speeding up changes within the organization, the development of regional networks and improvements in workplace representation. Now the *Health and Safety* project with IMF is expected to result in having three union experts in SIER who will be able to act as union inspectors and to help health and safety representatives in the companies in their work.

Finally, the results of union education are not simply 'downwards', i.e. transferring ideas and information to affiliates, but are also 'upwards', making significant transfers in the opposite direction, to the internationals. Union education cannot be seen as uni-directional learning whereby trade unionists at 'lower' levels learn from those at national and international levels. Labour educators themselves have unfortunately done little to dispel this misconception. Thus, otherwise excellent works produced by experienced practitioners simply deal with what union activists learn (see for example Spencer, 2002). Internationals can access both industrial relations and organisational information in this way, use it to relate closely to the unions' specific concerns and objective situations, and convey it to other unions. As we explained in Chapter three, education historically was the way that the internationals acquired vital information that allowed them to affiliate, assimilate and develop unions as they expanded outside of their strongholds in the developed world. Without such long-term, patient development of relationships this knowledge could not have been established and needs could not have been addressed in effective and efficient ways.

International union education has probably been most successful where unions from small groups of countries have been brought together with some external input. The model has shown itself to be more successful than simply bringing in external tutors or facilitators from developed countries to conduct courses. Strong examples of such groupings have existed in both francophone and anglophone West Africa, Ukraine and Moldova, the Scandinavian countries and the countries of central Asia. An obvious advantage has been to reduce the linguistic and other practical difficulties referred to in the previous chapter. In addition, the format allowed a focus on exchanging experience within a set of cognate problematics since institutional and cultural environments show a combination of commonality and readily recognised differences. A limited amount of external input by GUF representatives and foreign tutors has in these cases allowed a wider perspective when necessary.

An example is a small union in Tanzania, TAMICO, with members in the mining sector. As a result of the local system of 'African socialism' or 'Ujamaa' entailing state–union cooperation, the union had no history of organising workers. In 2001 a team of four organisers was established from the National Union of Mineworkers of South Africa. This exchange was facilitated by the ICEM through a regional shop stewards programme funded by Nordic donors and coordinated by Zimbabweans. The NUM organisers focussed on the Geita Mine, with approximately 3,000 workers, none of whom were unionised. Within two weeks, using South African experience and assistance, TAMICO had recruited 400 members. The ICEM helped the newly established branch and shop stewards to register the union and train its leaders. The union was able to make this dramatic shift in orientation through targeted contact with another mining union in the region and coordination with its international.

Education's Political Marginalisation

Educational activity is important to the internationals, yet as we have shown above, its funding is problematic because it comes from a small group of European countries with an increasing predilection for bilateral projects that bypass the internationals. At the same time, there has been a long-term shift away from discussing trade union education within the GUFs. The subject is dealt with in a cursory way within executive bodies. Since these problems exist in a major area of work, why are they not discussed more extensively? More broadly, why is education marginalised both in intra-GUF and academic discussion?

Education was regarded by a previous generation of experienced international trade unionists as a tool of self-evident use in their work. Omer Bécu, general secretary of the ICFTU, underlined its significance in his preface to Hans Gottfurcht's mid-1960s book on the history and current position of the international movement, a work whose main text also takes the importance of education as obvious (Bécu, 1966). Bécu describes it as 'indispensable for the firm anchoring of the trade unions in the developing world' (Bécu, 1966: 5). This recognition appears to have diminished since that time, and the assumption is that education is now conducted simply because it is requested and/or because it provides funds.

We suggest that there are two core reasons for this neglect. The first is that for many trade unions the activity is invisible, because it only applies to those most in need of it and therefore does not touch the relatively powerful and much-researched unions of the USA and Western Europe. Many large OECD-based trade unions affiliated to GUFs simply have no contact with the GUFs' education programmes. At any one time, at least 60 per cent of affiliates will not have international trade union education in their consciousness. Only the donor and recipient country affiliates will have any real understanding of what work is being conducted and its results.

The second reason is the more profound problem of demonstrating palpable outcomes from educational work. Often, very little baseline information is available about the unions involved prior to projects starting. For projects begun in the 1980s and 1990s, it was impossible to secure this information and there was therefore an almost complete absence of data about what these unions could already do. Moreover, although in many cases projects build organisational capacity and lead directly to recruiting new members, many of the results are vital intangibles such as building confidence in key activists. Impacts are also often indicated in only indirect ways – for example the successful completion of a negotiation process, which will always have other factors determining the outcomes.

Attempts to use indicators that take full account of intangibles can also bring problems with donors because they are in stark contrast to those that governments find acceptable. Increasingly, governments have sought to impose 'Logical Framework Analysis', a highly formulaic approach to planning and project management, on local unions. Global unions are consequently often caught between donors and unions as 'interpreters', trying to bring these two different languages and orientations into a meaningful dialogue. They have not always succeeded, and these approaches have alienated many unions in the developing world in addition to the GUFs.

Marginalisation of debate around education heightens the risk that it will fall by the wayside, and be displaced by bilateral activity. Schwass evokes a very real and sobering prospect:

> the future of trade union development cooperation looks bleak. If donors chose the easy way out by going bilateral, i.e. disregard GUFs as partners and work directly with national centres and unions in developing countries, then a lot of added value is lost. It would be the end of meaningful international trade union development cooperation.

> (Schwass, 2004: 23–4)

This is a crucial and timely point made when donors under pressure to report results to their governments on an annual basis may find it easier to carry out bilateral programmes with national unions or NGOs. Development funds set up to build unions would then have no genuine link to the collective experience of decades of trade union education carried out through the internationals, a bleak prospect for donors and recipient organisations alike.

Herein may lie the final reason for the marginalisation of education within the internationals: the very difficulty of the issue and lack of any obvious or immediate solutions leads to denial because they do not feel that they can address such a large-scale problem.

The Education–Research Symbiosis

Research is a function that also suffers from restricted discussion within the internationals. It is a function with a number of different uses and has considerable symbiotic potential with the educational approach. Yet the current research deficit means that the GUFs are under-equipped with the results of dedicated research that can provide them with the tools they need to make well-supported arguments and buttress their positions as sectoral experts.

Research on companies can obviously yield significant results for unions, revealing how corporations interlink, their ownership, supply chains, stakeholder structures and so on. Greven (2008: 2) argues that 'solidly based sophisticated' research on industrial sectors is essential to US-style strategic campaigning against corporations that identifies all the pressure points that may be accessed to pressurise them, and his argument holds equally for organising or collective bargaining. In addition, detailed and properly contextualised accounts of how unions have developed their own organisation to approach key problems have great potential. These can be fed into courses, but can also be developed from them. Much rich discussion held inside classrooms draws on unique experience that cannot be accessed by other means and this needs to be captured for the use of other trade unionists.

Many small or workplace-based unions have little or no research capacity, yet most of the GUFs themselves carry out little more than the simplest forms of investigation, providing too little detail and analysis for them to be of great use to affiliates. Research for the European Industry Federations, on the other hand, is relatively well developed, partly because researchers in Europe themselves have the capacity to work without a great deal of funding from the Federations. A good example is that of the European Institute for Construction Labour Research, which has existed for over fifteen years and publishes the widely distributed and well-regarded *CLR News*. Similarly, the great majority of OECD unions have both their own research departments and good links to academic networks.

The few examples of effective use of research demonstrate its potential. The ITF carries out research on key logistics companies, circulating it widely; similarly, its case studies on organising in the informal economy show the possibilities of transferring significant experience in this way (Bonner, 2006). High-quality research is also produced for one relatively well-resourced GUF, the PSI, to underpin its anti-privatisation campaigning. The PSI Research Unit based at the University of Greenwich in London produces a steady stream of reports and publications that help provide solid data to support the PSI's campaigning.

The ITGLWF developed multilevel research on companies it targeted in the early 2000s. 'Multilevel' because it involved trade unionists at different levels in companies investigating both their operations and the company's suppliers fully. Miller (2004) provides a striking example of the combination of education, research and determined local organising activity that brought positive results in the Southern African clothing industry. Activists were trained, and research conducted in Southern Africa was used to identify the primary contractors of Asian MNCs exploiting the US Africa Growth and Opportunity Act in the Maseru Export Processing Zone. This was in turn used to exert pressure on the US companies ordering the goods, with the result that one-third of the 26 companies in membership of the Lesotho Textile Exporters' Association conceded union recognition to some degree.

It might be suggested that research capacity of the required type does in fact exist, in the form of the Global Union Research Network (GURN). This was established to try and bridge the gap between unions and academics, notably by coordinating the ILO and academics to generate dedicated research. It brought together a group of supportive academics and research institutions worldwide but the results have been small in relation to GUFs' needs. In addition, donors are increasingly funding research, such as that carried out by the Observatório Social in Brazil, but without union involvement or developing union capacity to carry out their own research.

The need is for dedicated researchers to work on a GUF by GUF basis, with increased resources. GUFs require databases of supply chains and collective agreements, but unions will not provide these for public display on the web. In educational contexts, high-trust relations can be built, allowing exchange of relatively sensitive documents of this type. As Miller shows, educational approaches can make a further contribution by developing research capacity in local activists through a mix of classroom-based and coaching activities.

Conclusion

Vitally, it has a democratising effect within unions, from which the internationals have already benefited, raising the participants' levels of commitment to operating within existing structures. Much academic discussion of union renewal all too often misses the essential processes of human interaction and development that necessarily underpin any such renewal. These are enhanced by education. But slow, patient work developing activists through long-term education programmes and informal dialogue does not hit any headlines and is currently under-discussed both in the internationals and more widely. It is nevertheless a significant aspect of efforts to raise the level of contact between the world's unions and to improve their effectiveness. Vitally, it has a democratising effect within unions, from which the internationals have already benefited, raising the participants' levels of commitment to operating within existing structures.

We advocate further expanding this type of work. Yet the intermittent and precarious resources available to the GUFs for education are under threat and constitute a problem requiring full discussion. The internationals' reliance on donors' funds for developmental work masks the reluctance of national unions in developed countries to pay anything more than relatively small amounts to international bodies, as discussed in Chapter four. This is an immediate problem and the signs of change are currently running in the wrong direction. Swedish unions, previously highly reliable contributors to educational projects are now seeking to minimise their overall financial contribution. The problem is as serious as the dues income problem outlined earlier and similarly requires an open political discussion between unions about whether they are prepared to make the necessary investment in international work.

CHAPTER EIGHT

Case Study – a GUF's Relationship with a Multinational Company

Introduction

THIS chapter illustrates many of the themes developed and discussed earlier. It is a case study of the ICEM's relationship with Anglo American plc (AA), analysing how the GUF, national unions in South Africa, Ghana and Colombia and the company interacted with positive results for workers. The main institutional players are represented in Diagram 4.

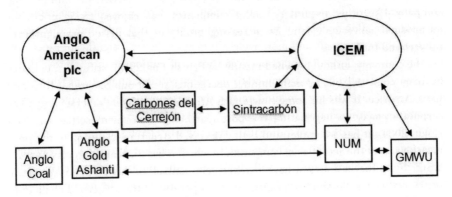

Diagram 4: Anglo American and its Relationships to other Main Players

The case was selected for two reasons. First, it was chosen because *prima facie* it allowed detailed examination of how a GUF acted as a major player in advancing workers' interests. Second, unusually high-quality longitudinal information was obtained through the long-term involvement of one of the authors, supplemented by extensive project reports, company and union documentation.

We show how the GUF developed a positive relationship with a multinational by integrative bargaining on an issue of great significance both to it and to workers; this built company consent for distributive bargaining by affiliates in a different part of its operation on another continent. The narrative demonstrates the significance of strong articulation developed over many years between the national and international union levels, in part created and supported by a strong educational input. The GUF's role was crucial: none of the national unions in the case had previously related effectively to multinationals. The GUF learned from the process and transferred the approach elsewhere in the world. The case confirms that, contrary to Neuhaus' (1981) suggestion, GUFs can initiate significant developments and need not simply react to other actors' agendas.

The case is presented in three sections. The first introduces the company and its relationship with the ICEM. The second analyses work developed in Ghana around HIV/AIDS in the mining sector. The third section examines the dynamics of rebuilding union dialogue with mining companies in Colombia. Finally, we draw broad conclusions and examine the case's wider relevance.

The Company, the ICEM, National Trade Unions and Their Relationships

Anglo American is one of the world's largest corporations, ranked 88 in the Financial Times Stock Exchange index of the world's largest 500 companies and employing 162,000 people worldwide in 2006. Its operations are focussed on mining. The company, like other natural resources companies, has enjoyed rising prices for its products since 2000, and its increasing profits in that period are significant background to the case.

The company, although owned mainly by British financial institutions, operates in many countries but its main mining operations are in Sub-Saharan Africa and Latin America. It was for some time South Africa's largest conglomerate and a key corporate player in negotiating the post-apartheid employment settlement (von Holdt, 2004). It has a complex and highly devolved structure, claiming in response to criticisms of the activities of companies in which it has a sizeable interest (War on Want, 2007) that it does not have 'management control' of them (Anglo American, 2007). Following the practice of many such corporations, the associated companies have high levels of managerial autonomy and seek to establish internal leadership in both efficiency and CSR matters. In this sense it is typical of the modern multinational, and can be conceived of as a 'federation' (Andersson et al., 2007) or a grouping of companies linked by a range of methods including overlapping directorships and shareholdings. The overall company composition in 2004 is portrayed in Table 14.

It is clear from Table 14 that in 2004 it had a controlling financial interest in both Anglo Coal and Anglo Gold Ashanti (AGA). This interest was reduced to 41.8 per cent in April 2006; but until spring 2007, AA retained two directors on the AGA board. In 2000, AA bought a 33 per cent share in the Cerrejón mine in Colombia; by

2006 three companies, AA, BHP Billiton and Xstrata, were equal shareholders. AA works closely with Cerrejón management.

Table 14: Anglo American plc – Business Overview, 2004

Business Area	Main Countries of Operation	Key Subsidiaries	Percentage Ownership of Subsidiaries
Platinum	South Africa	Anglo Platinum	74.1%
Gold	South Africa	Anglo Gold Ashanti	54.5% (17% in 2008)
Diamonds	South Africa	De Beers	45%
Coal	South Africa, Colombia	Anglo Coal	100%
Base Metals	Chile	Anglo Base Metals	100%
Industrial Minerals	UK, France, Belgium	Anglo Industrial Minerals	100%
Paper and Packaging	South Africa, Russia	Anglo Paper and Packaging	100%
Ferrous Metals and Industries	South Africa, Australia	Anglo Ferrous Metals and Industries	100%

Source: Anglo American plc, *The Business: An Overview*, 14 February 2004

Company relations with stakeholders have to be built on a long-term basis, Sir Mark Moody-Stuart, chairman, argued to shareholders at the April 2008 AGM. Fixed sites and high front-end expenditure mean 'that we have to live with the judgements we make about our ability to operate ethically in particular locations' (Anglo American, 2008). 'Resource nationalism' increasingly means the company has to attend to its wider political profile throughout its operations. AA and AGA are highly engaged with international development and since 2000 AA has made a considerable contribution to the UK government's Africa strategy. The company's CSR efforts are also reflected in its role in establishing and building the Global Business Coalition (GBC), set up to promote business responses to HIV/AIDS, which Sir Mark Moody-Stuart chairs. The GBC claims that it has supported millions of people through implementing local workplace programmes with its 220 member companies.

AA has taken a 'business case' approach to HIV/AIDS provision, although there is considerable congruence between business and CSR rationales. AA's subsidiary Anglo Coal was one of the first companies in the world to calculate the precise economic benefits of providing antiretrovirals (ARVs), but this 'making disease management pay' (the phrase is that of Dr Richard Gaunt (2007) of AA's major competitor Rio Tinto) approach is becoming well established in mining companies. Research carried out in Anglo Coal showed in 2006 that it was economic to provide private medical insurance, including possible VCT and ARVs, for all employees and their dependents rather than to provide nothing. The company's preliminary cost-benefit analysis is shown in Table 15 below. After the first year, the costs of providing drugs were estimated to decline relative to savings from absenteeism and healthcare. This calculation accompanied a move beyond the classic position taken by companies, whereby they deny any legal responsibility for workers' sexual health. The latter position clearly rejects any real responsibility for reducing risk, in order to limit potential liabilities (Weait, 2007).

Table 15: Anglo Coal – Preliminary Cost Benefit Analysis of Providing ART

Duration	ART Cost per Month (Rands)	Absenteeism Savings per Month	Health Care Cost Saving
Per month saved vs no ART – 12 months	R2223	R1052	R755
Per month saved vs no ART – 18 months	R1652	R1093	R804
Per month saved vs no ART – 24 months	R1304	R1126	R837
Additional saved CD4 100–250 vs less than 100 – Two years pre-positive		R458	R396

Source: Ms D. Muirhead, Aurum Institute for Health Research, presentation
(Document in authors' possession)

The company has scope and reasons for improving both its health and safety record and its public image: in 2007 it reported that forty-four people were killed in its mining operations, and its practices in relation to indigenous communities have been sharply criticised (War on Want, 2007). Part of its reply to War on Want's criticisms was to point to its record in publicly insisting that the Colombian government attend to the physical defence of trade unionists. Like many mining employers, AA is reconciled to trade unionism and almost all of its mining sites have a major union presence. The company has sought to construct positive relations with unions, including them in efforts to improve efficiency by cost reduction; union cooperation in health and safety has brought major benefits to the rate of return on capital employed. Their experience at the New Denmark mine in South Africa demonstrated this dramatically, when union partnership helped raise the return on capital employed from 24.7 per cent in 2001 to 43.2 per cent in 2003. Moody-Stuart used this experience as a model for others in the company to follow (Anglo American, 2003). Hence, the links between trade unionism, health and safety and profitability are well recognised at the top of the company.

Anglo Gold has robust long-term relations with the South African National Union of Mineworkers (NUM), based on AA's 'progressive positions' on recognising black unions in South Africa, and its part in the transition to democracy (Anglo American, 2003; 2008). The NUM itself had a central role in ending apartheid and enjoys great prestige within the trade union movement both in Africa and internationally, with strong bilateral links with other mining unions, and high-profile participation in the ICEM and the IMF. The NUM has long emphasised HIV/AIDS as an issue, having concluded an agreement with the South African Chamber of Mines on the subject in 1993 (N'Deba and Hodges-Aeberhard, 1998). The union has a broad political conception of its representative functions and has successfully negotiated protection for contract workers (von Holdt and Webster, 2005). The NUM has conducted personnel exchanges with many African mining unions and has had a long-term relationship with the Ghana Mineworkers' Union (GMWU) based on personal contacts developed through the ICEM Regional Committee. The GMWU is itself a strong union within the well-developed Ghanaian trade union movement (Frazer, 2008), and is therefore a relatively equal partner for the NUM. It is a highly politicised organisation, focussed on dialogue with the state which until recently ran the mines. It was only therefore relatively recently that the GMWU had to negotiate with private management and the union stood to learn from a relationship with the NUM.

Exchanges between the ICEM and AA were partly based on the long-standing relationship between Fred Higgs (then ICEM general secretary, retired 2006) and Sir Mark Moody-Stuart. The two were in contact when Moody-Stuart held management positions at Royal Dutch Shell and Higgs was National Oil Industry Officer at the UK's Transport and General Workers' Union. This contact continued through difficult years for Shell and for oil workers, including the 1995 Brent Spar incident. The relationship was renewed through their joint participation in the United Nations Global Compact's Advisory Committee from that body's foundation in 2002. The committee was established to help the Global Compact develop speedily into a credible CSR mechanism, working directly under Kofi Annan's office at the United Nations. Its membership included representatives of civil society, labour (GUFs and the ITUC) and business. Shortly after its creation, Moody-Stuart became AA chairman but retained his Advisory Committee position. The foundations of trust between Higgs and Moody-Stuart were built on the fact that, unlike other participants, both came from an industrial relations background. They held similar views on the minimum 'integrity measures' that would be credible for the Global Compact to be an effective body, based on their experience of industrial monitoring and complaints procedures. Their capacity for joint action was higher than either had with the non-governmental organisations involved.

There was also a long term and complex web of relationships between the ICEM and its key affiliate the NUM, and of both with the CEO of Anglo Gold Ashanti,

Bobby Godsell. Godsell is an exceptional business person. On his retirement from the company in 2008, he was credited by Moody-Stuart with a significant role in South Africa's transition to democracy (Anglo American, 2008). An industrial relations expert, he was hailed as an 'organic intellectual' of South African business (Handley, 2005) for his part in South Africa's transition. The editor of works on South Africa's future (Berger and Godsell, 1988), he persuaded a sceptical business community of the merits of the Labour Relations Act in its amended 2002 version, which improved legal cover for contract workers (Bidoli, 2004). In 2002, he surprised a business meeting in New York by wearing an NUM strike T-shirt (*ibid.*). Godsell had a close relationship with Cyril Ramaphosa, the first NUM president and subsequent secretary general of the ANC who became chairman of the Mondi paper and packaging group after its de-merger from AA (Bidoli, 2004; Mondi, 2007).

In West Africa, long-term relationships also existed between AGA management and medical staff, the ICEM and the Ghana Mineworkers' Union (GMWU). The GMWU president, John Brimpong, was the Ghana TUC's HIV/AIDS representative, and a member of the ICEM regional and international executives who was well known both within Ghanaian mining communities and to local mine management. Brimpong was at the centre of a constellation of industry and community contacts built up over forty years of union activity. An already close relationship between GMWU leadership, the ICEM and senior AGA medical staff was cemented through the latter's HIV/AIDS project.

The ICEM's HIV/AIDS Pilot Projects: Background and Significance

The ICEM was one of the first GUFs, with ITF and EI, to take a lead on promoting HIV/AIDS action by unions since workers in these sectors are disproportionately affected. From 2002 the ICEM worked with affiliates to develop a strategy and initial activity. The union problems identified when dealing with HIV/AIDS were defined as lack of leadership, the stigma around testing and a lack of sustainable funding for treatment. An additional barrier in Africa was the reluctance of workplace representatives, often from Christian backgrounds, to confront the issue. At that point virtually no ICEM affiliate, except those in South Africa, Ghana and Botswana, recognised HIV/AIDS as a union issue. In countries outside Africa, ICEM affiliates, notably in Eastern Europe, strongly resisted the argument. The African affiliates could therefore potentially become international leaders to persuade others of the case for taking up the area of work.

Following six months of consultation with affiliates already active around the issue and experienced HIV/AIDS activists, the ICEM and these affiliates decided to promote medical provision and prevention programmes, and to negotiate anti-discrimination policies through pilot schemes that could later be adopted elsewhere in the world. The agenda was therefore more ambitious than the earlier common union practice of simply carrying out awareness campaigns. It entailed developing core expertise, raising funds from new sources and dialogue with both employers and government.

HIV/AIDS is a central labour management concern for multinationals invested in Africa and Eastern Europe. In Sub-Saharan mining, infection rates are approximately double national averages and frequently higher. In Zambia the BBC reports a national infection rate of 14 per cent, and an estimated 50 per cent in mining communities (BBC News Online, published 22/06/2006). These high rates are explained by four factors. The first is the remoteness of mining operations and the communities surrounding them. Second, single sex workers' hostels, although reducing in number, are widespread. Third, many male migrant and contract workers are away from their partners, further stimulating high levels of prostitution and 'second families'. Fourth, stigma and denial around sexual practice and prevention of infection is widespread.

The private sector plays a significant role in general healthcare in these communities, making miners dependent on companies for health, and in some cases life, as well as work. The majority of clinics and hospitals in mining regions are to some extent privately supported or funded. Most miners working directly for multinationals at present are members of private medical insurance schemes which provide antiretroviral drugs, although this is a recent development and rarely applies to indirect or contract workers. Thus, companies play a considerable role in the diagnosis of HIV/AIDS and in providing access to treatment as well as in healthcare more broadly.

The diagnosis of HIV/AIDS raises significant dilemmas for management and workplace representatives alike and is therefore extremely demanding for individuals on both personal and professional levels. If a worker with HIV/AIDS is threatened with dismissal, this raises fundamental issues about that worker's future. Workers' fear of losing their jobs demands strong workplace representation by the union, since local management may take action against them despite statements by senior company staff thousands of miles away. The issue giving rise to the dismissal threat may not be the simple fact of the worker having HIV/AIDS. For example, a worker receiving antiretrovirals through a company medical scheme may face dismissal for a gross misconduct matter. The local manager and workplace representative will both have to take personal responsibility for evaluating the cost to the worker, his family and the community of him losing his job and, simultaneously, his access to treatment.

Workers must be convinced that testing will not lead to dismissal and, to a lesser degree, they also must be confident that it will lead to treatment. This should be seen in the context that until legislation changed in 2003, mining companies in South Africa practised compulsory testing for workers at the point of recruitment, refusing those who tested positive (Kenny, 2004). The role of trade unions is important in negotiating, verifying and rigorously policing any assurances by securing anti-discrimination and anti-victimisation protections in collective agreements, promoting and monitoring VCT provision and by convincing workers that they will not suffer if tested.

Most workers, even in highly infected areas do not present themselves for testing. Only tiny percentages of workers normally volunteer, particularly if testing is offered by company doctors in company facilities. Companies draw a distinction between confidential and anonymous testing, arguing that they practise the latter, but this fails to reassure workers. Most employees in African mining companies have limited confidence in management's concern for their interests (von Holdt, 2004) and they require credible guarantees of protection from company action against them that only union involvement can offer.

Preparing for and Implementing the Projects

In September 2002, on the ICEM's initiative, an International Framework Agreement was signed between Anglo Gold, ICEM and the NUM, the first such agreement signed with a company operating in Africa. The accord was signed in public after the UN's World Summit in South Africa, and promoted as part of the company's sustainable development work. It had essentially symbolic rather than substantive significance in tackling HIV/AIDS, because it contains no clause on the subject. It nevertheless symbolically cemented the relations between the three signatories and was relevant background to their cooperation in the HIV/AIDS field.

By 2004 the ICEM had launched an international HIV/AIDS initiative, designed to identify pilot workplaces where the GUF and its affiliates could develop workplace provision, with the support of employers, local hospitals and international funding. The project aimed to mainstream the issue in affiliates' policies and practice. It was decided to work in two Ghanaian mining regions, Obuasi and Tarkwa, with Anglo Gold Ashanti and its partner company with which it was merged in April 2004, Ashanti Goldfields, because of the working relationship with the companies and the GMWU's clear commitment to conduct the demanding programme. Overall, the project worked within the comprehensive guidance offered by the ILO Code of Practice on HIV/AIDS in the Workplace; the immediate objective was to implement a strategy based on the Code. The pilot project aimed to secure, through negotiations with these key employers, the establishment or development of dedicated medical facilities for VCT and treatment, and adequate anti-discrimination and non-victimisation clauses in agreements. The pilots would in due course identify other important needs, including a need for trained peer counsellors from union cadres to support miners diagnosed positive. These counsel people before and after testing, helping them to make lifestyle changes and to manage their treatment.

These companies, unlike many others, have professional staff to manage HIV/AIDS to high technical standards. By 2004 the ICEM also had acquired dedicated HIV/AIDS coordinators. The experts responsible for CSR and HIV/AIDS in both the company and the GUF facilitated technical discussion between the partners. Technical staff involvement also helped build consensus within the companies since there was marked management resistance within them, as in other companies, to acquiring inherently difficult and open-ended responsibilities which generate considerable uncertainty about future costs and requirements. For all parties involved, there is no margin for error. Even small technical mistakes in HIV/AIDS testing and treatment programmes are likely to reduce uptake and to make restoring miners' confidence very difficult.

It has been suggested that the most effective company strategy is to carry out in-house programmes, without involving partners (Husted, 2003). Yet the AA companies rejected this option. Company engagement with the GUF and local unions occurred against the background of strong relationships outlined above, but its immediate cause was the practical issue of testing and the positive effect that the company felt the union could have. The huge scope for charismatic union leaders to influence workers' perceptions is difficult to envisage outside of the African mining context. Their role is highly significant well beyond the workplace, since they are seen as community, and not simply as workplace, leaders. This influence has frequently been referred to by AA managers. Thus, Brian Brink, AA's senior vice-president for health, highlighted the partnership with other organisations including unions as 'crucial to success' in tackling HIV/AIDS (Business Action in Africa, 2007: 20).

Senzeni Zokwana, the president of the NUM (elected president of the ICEM at its Bangkok Congress in 2007) personally took the issue of HIV/AIDS to mines. He carried out awareness raising activities and encouraged testing. He publicly submitted himself for personal testing at each mine, paving the way for successful testing drives. The union also undertook a wider educational effort to train peer educators and negotiators to bargain for protections for people living with HIV/AIDS.

HIV/AIDS programmes are often reported in vague ways, but in the cases of AGA and AA more widely, tangible results could be reported. In AGA in 2004, 10 per cent of employees were being tested; in the company's 2006 annual report, 75 per cent were reported as having been tested. By June 2006 34 per cent of AA's workers had been tested: 9,758 of an estimated positive work force of 28,294 were enrolled in the company's HIV/AIDS programme, 3,772 of whom were taking up antiretroviral treatment. In comparative terms, these are high take-up rates and a significant improvement on previous levels.

A further concrete result is identifiable, since the Ghana pilots triggered agreements with the employer and government. AGA signed a public–private partnership agreement with the Ghanaian Ministry of Health in 2005 to provide

HIV/AIDS testing and treatment and malaria control in the Obuasi mining area, an initiative supported by the ICEM. In this 'co-investment' project (Vuckvic et al., 2005), the company donates the infrastructure of the hospital and available medical staff. It provides VCT and ART to its employees and their dependents at these facilities through an agreement with the Ghanaian government and with insurance company funding.

The project provided an essential first step in establishing the possibility of moving beyond an awareness-raising model by making material progress and showing concretely how that could be done. It also made the case to companies outside those directly involved that union cooperation is a positive factor. The pilot initiative has been exported, at the time of writing, to other companies in Ghana and also to Botswana, Nigeria, Namibia, Democratic Republic of Congo, Côte d'Ivoire and Mali.

We now turn to the second element of the case study: ICEM–union–company relationships at the Cerrejón mine in Colombia.

Colombia

This part of the study focuses on relations between the Sintracarbón union and Carbones del Cerrejón, part owned by AA. As indicated above, AA is closely involved in Cerrejón with regular visits to the mine by senior AA staff including Edward Bickham, executive vice president, external affairs. The African initiatives described above were essential background to developments in Colombia since they created awareness within the GUF and the company that positive relations on that continent were yielding benefits for both sides. It also shows how education played a significant role in building relationships between Colombian unions and generating union capacity to act locally in relation to AA and other companies.

For trade unionists, Colombia has long represented the most dangerous country in the world. The civil war has placed unions in a highly vulnerable position since they have to operate with and in the interstices between government, guerrillas, paramilitary forces, multinationals and criminals (Pearce, 2004). Hundreds of union leaders have been assassinated during the last decade, causing activists to reduce or abandon their union work, leaving small, isolated unions. At the time of writing, many trade unionists have again been forced into hiding by a wave of violence.

Overcoming Problems of Inter-union Dialogue

Colombian unions have varied and powerful political orientations that tend to fragment them. Unions in the ICEM sectors are affiliated to the main centre-left Colombian union federation, Central Unitaria de Trabajadores (CUT). They have a strong orientation towards political action, and the state has the legal right to intervene in their affairs. Up until 2000, none of the unions discussed below provided representative services to members and had only minimal experience of collective bargaining, while some resisted dialogue with employers on political grounds. Certain unions actively supported oppositional movements while others retained their historical basis in left-wing groups although there is no organisational or political link between the unions and the left-wing guerrilla organisations ELN or FARC. One union was built from the radical M19 grouping, although M19 was disbanded and no longer directs union strategy. Unions have strong factional dynamics and most unions experience mistrust between executive members that becomes acute at high points in the societal conflict.

Unions in the ICEM's industries also have significant industrial differences. For example the Sintraelecol union is a large public sector union, with the highest level of security threat for union leadership. Miners, among the first Colombian workers to organise in the early twentieth century, have a respected position, but are also exposed in relation to threats of violence against them. Sintraquim, by contrast, is a small, relatively moderate union representing a majority of women working in the chemicals and pharmaceuticals sectors, mainly concerned with the lack of secure jobs and factory closures. These differences make it difficult for unions to cooperate, both between themselves but also within the CUT and the ICEM. This reinforces their sense of isolation and weakness in relation to employers. It should be noted however that the ICEM affiliates have attempted to work in a coordinated way for ten years as the ICEM Colombia Committee, which reflects their increasingly important positioning within CUT and, more recently, with employers.

The ICEM's Interventions

The foundations of the ICEM's work were educational, and projects moved through three overlapping stages: building the GUF–union relationship, reviewing the unions' own structures and ways of working and finally bargaining with companies.

The ICEM's work with Colombian unions began in the 1980s through the Education Department of the Miners' International Federation (MIF), which merged with ICEF in 1995 to form the ICEM. Ann Browne, then MIF education officer, established contacts with the mining unions, initially informally, focussing on mining communities and child labour, which were priority issues for the MIF at that point. These contacts led to a relationship with the current leadership of the Sintracarbón (at that time Sintraintercor) union.

Sintracarbón and the Carbones del Cerrejón management were central to wider developments in Colombia. The Cerrejón mine is one of the largest open caste coal mines in the world and Sintracarbón is also an important ICEM affiliate. Its president, Jaime Deluquez, is a member of both the ICEM Latin American regional committee and its international executive committee. He is a well respected and highly effective member of the international with a deep awareness of the possibilities and limits of international trade unionism, formulating clear requests to the ICEM and its affiliates in ways that could be readily understood and responded to. He is therefore in a strong position to represent the interests of his own union and the other ICEM Colombian affiliates at international level. His reputation with management was that of a capable and focussed leader. He played a key role in helping build the relationships between Sintracarbón, Carbones del Cerrejón and the ICEM.

In 1975 the state-owned company Carbones de Colombia (Carbocol) sold 50 per cent of the Cerrejón mine to Intercor, an ExxonMobil subsidiary. In the late 1990s the mine and the surrounding region suffered from poor health and safety conditions and in response to Colombian requests were included in the MIF's international Health and Safety Project for mining unions. Interestingly, the GMWU also participated in this successful global health and safety project. The project, in addition to campaigning for ratification of the ILO's mining safety convention, C.176, provided education and consultancies for unions to develop their own health and safety capacity and to work with managements to build medical services. Significant gains were made by the union, including introducing the first occupational health testing system in the mine and creating a good working relationship with company medical staff. The doctor currently in charge of the Cerrejón medical facilities, Dr Salvador Uricoechea, first met the union through this programme. Uricoechea and the union established comprehensive systems for data collection and testing for occupational diseases.

This programme ended in 1998 and simultaneously a dedicated educational methods programme began, for ICEM affiliates in Colombia and those interested in affiliating. The consistent funding and support it received for fifteen years from the Swedish metal and mining union Metall (now IFMetall) and LO-TCO was essential. From 1998 until 2004 the programme was coordinated from Bogotá by the experienced trade unionist Carlos Bustos. The high-quality work focussed on educational methods for Colombian regional and national leaders, with particular emphasis on providing a safe and inclusive educational environment for national and local leaders. The project funded them to travel by air rather than by the inherently dangerous road routes and provided an important way for national leaders to meet their own regional and local activists.

Union educational methods provided democratic and safe contexts for trade unionists to debate and find solutions to highly threatening problems. The educational setting provides clear rules and participation, and emphasises equality between participants – exceptional emphases in the national context. For those that came from a highly politicised background, the experience of participatory education was initially very difficult to come to terms with, as they were accustomed to lecture-based, and position-taking modes of exchange. At first, classroom discussions were highly combative, leading to absenteeism. Less senior, female and younger trade unionists were initially unwilling to participate in joint activities, but this changed as the focus gradually shifted from aggressive political debate towards finding practical and practicable joint solutions to industrial relations problems.

Over time, participants grew to appreciate the educational environment, and the removal of restrictions and stress when they attended project activities. Attendance gradually improved. For many involved, the risks of congregating in one location meant that for attendance at project activities to be so consistent over the long term the benefits must have been significant. Education provided an opportunity to build social capital: friendships and good working relationships were formed between activists from the same and different unions. This had a long term effect on their behaviour at ICEM and other union events and also provided them with a firm social base from which to venture into trying to address their individual unions' ways of working. By 2004 the ICEM's six affiliates were all prepared to start reviewing their organisations.

A new phase of education was therefore directed at examining these issues. The unions perceived their problems to be recruiting new members, weak finances, corruption, and lack of education at any level, all contributing to organisational stagnation. Both joint and single union seminars were carried out using ICEM staff to initiate thinking around organisational change, focussing in particular on the difficult recruitment issue. Although this phase was relatively short, the discussions stimulated union executives to think beyond the immediate crisis that they faced, to consider longer-term objectives and to regard the possibilities of recruitment more positively. In brief, they began to take a more strategic approach, including in terms of their relations with employers.

Dialogue with Employers

A final phase of the ICEM's educational work in Colombia turned to the core issue of dialogue with employers. By 2003 collective bargaining had effectively atrophied. Colombian law allows management and unions to extend collective bargaining agreements without revision at six monthly intervals, and the practice had become common. The level of danger for union leaderships is raised during negotiations with management, discouraging negotiators from resuming discussions. The education programme was redirected towards a process of formally denominated social dialogue, directly mediated by the ICEM, involving the six ICEM affiliates and eight nominated MNCs.

The original MNCs identified were:

- Anglo American (UK)
- BHP Billiton (Australia)
- Xstrata (Switzerland)
- Linde (Germany)
- Codensa/Endesa (Spain)

- Owens Illinois (USA)
- Smurfitt (Ireland)
- Union FENOSA (Spain).

The related ICEM affiliates were:

- Sintraelecol (Elecric Power)
- Sintravidricol (Glass)
- Sintracarcol (Paper & Cardboard)
- Sintracarbón (Coal)
- Sintraquim (Chemicals & Pharmaceuticals)
- Fenaltec (Electrical Engineers).

One-day meetings occurred every quarter, preceded by ICEM affiliate meetings and facilitated by the ICEM leadership to agree areas for negotiation. Complementary research was commissioned by the ICEM on specific areas such as contract labour, and union-only and joint training activities were organised on new issues such as HIV/AIDS. The areas identified by the group for negotiation included security for trade unionists, health and safety, HIV/AIDS and contract labour.

A process of ICEM-mediated negotiations with employers was initiated around this agenda and carried on for several years with an increasing emphasis, encouraged by the ICEM, on bilateral negotiations between employers and unions. International mediation provided both sides with an externally created platform to restart direct collective bargaining. AA and the Spanish-owned utilities multinational Endesa (with whom the ICEM has an International Framework Agreement) were pivotal to company participants responding to central company prompting to become involved. The security and health and safety agendas were especially attractive to these companies.

A framework for dialogue was agreed in the early stages, designed to provide clear mechanisms for unions and employers. The central commitment of both the companies and union partners was to seek common ground and agreement. Importantly, the partners committed to participation in the process regardless of any local disputes or ongoing collective bargaining. Partners were asked to nominate formally a small team of representatives responsible for maintaining dialogue within their organisation. These were responsible for ensuring their consistent participation, for securing bilateral meetings at workplace level to debate areas of common interest, for maintaining regular communication with partners and the ICEM and finally for contacting the ICEM general secretary if difficulties arose. The importance of continuity of personnel from both unions and companies was emphasised, to ensure that momentum was maintained.

In 2004, the process, still at an early stage, was buttressed by state involvement. The government appears to have been interested in closer relations with companies, and in discussing human rights issues both with them and with the ICEM. Employer and union partners attended regular meetings with the Ministry for Social Protection, to present the issues under negotiation and seek support from the ministry for the principles of their work. The meetings were headed by Jorge León Sánchez, vice-minister for social protection, and his staff, joined initially by government human rights specialists. Areas for future work were identified including promoting HIV/AIDS initiatives and developing tripartite dialogue on setting limits and standards on contract and agency labour. Importantly, the vice-minister committed himself to prioritise action when unions approached the ministry about union representatives' security.

The most significant outcome of the ICEM programme was improved dialogue between Sintracarbón and Carbones del Cerrejón. On 1 December 2004 negotiations between Carbones del Cerrejón and Sintracarbón re-opened. The negotiations were closely watched by other companies and unions to see what could be achieved at a time when the level of violence against, and murder of, unionists was especially high. During the negotiation period the union negotiators and their families were threatened with extortion and assassination and the entire negotiating team was forced into hiding. Sintracarbón contacted the ICEM to inform them of the threats. The ICEM immediately contacted Sir Mark Moody-Stuart, and requested that they contact Cerrejón management to establish whether the company was in a position to minimise the risk. AA management and the union immediately issued a joint statement affirming their belief in fundamental labour rights and condemning intimidation. The company drew the threats to the attention of the vice president of Colombia, asking that the personal security of those involved be ensured. The negotiation process was able to continue; and although the threats did not entirely stop, they diminished and the negotiators and their families were unharmed throughout. Developing an HIV/AIDS pilot in the Cerrejón mine was discussed in 2006 with senior AA management as the final stage in this relationship. Although it is currently unclear whether this will succeed, it is testimony to the strength of relationships that such a complex issue could be broached in the context.

These negotiations brought some benefits for workers, and established a momentum that built on these. As a result of a subsequent wave of negotiations, an improved agreement was signed on 28 January 2007. The agreement brought salary increases for all workers including those in ancillary jobs and holding fixed-term contracts. The company pension scheme was opened for the first time to workers on fixed-term contracts of longer than six months. Also for the first time the company agreed to follow Colombian legislation by monitoring contract workers' conditions, and by jointly carrying out health and safety inspections within the mine with Sintracarbón representatives. In addition, the agreement covered social issues such as education and family benefits.

Sintracarbón's achievements provided motivation for other unions to embark on renewed collective bargaining. Thus, for example, coordinated bargaining was subsequently secured in the glass sector after many years of stalling by key employer Owens Illinois. The results of these negotiations were uneven, but overall workers' conditions were improved in both salary and health and safety terms. In companies where senior management had a strong relationship with the ICEM, local bargaining was more successful than elsewhere. Ensuring the participation of local management in most cases required direct communication between the ICEM Secretariat and the multinational's senior management. In these cases, they received unequivocal instruction from international and in some cases regional management to participate in good faith. Without this, it is unlikely that local managers would have participated as fully as they did.

The Colombian union movement itself remains both divided and fragile although currently the ICEM unions and their national centre, CUT, enjoy the highest level of internal cohesion in their history. Alliances between the ICEM unions involved have proved to be extremely strong, and they represent the most cohesive bloc within CUT. The unions are in regular contact with each other in relation to security for union leaders, contacts which were totally absent in the past. The CUT itself has improved its standing nationally and internationally and is recognised as a serious partner at both levels. All of this has provided a solid base for individual unions and raised their confidence in their capacity to deal with multinationals.

Without the many years of educational programmes, it is unlikely that the relationship between the ICEM and its affiliates would have developed sufficiently strongly to sustain a difficult, complex and prolonged process of internationally mediated negotiations. The ICEM's direct role in preparing unions and creating new spaces for dialogue created the only opportunity the unions had to step outside a previously intractable dynamic of threats and local disputes. The Colombian experience of social dialogue was consciously adopted and systematically transferred by the ICEM to other situations such as Thailand and Peru where dialogue between unions and employers had broken down.

We have to record here the torture and murder of Adolfo González Montes, a Sintracarbón leader at his home on 22 March 2008. Adolfo's murder reminds us of the continued risks faced by trade unionists in that country.

Conclusion

The GUF leveraged a 'partnership' approach in one part of the company's operation to enable a revival of distributive bargaining in another. The company was prepared to offset the clear efficiency advantages which it won from raising workers' participation in HIV/AIDS programmes in Africa against the costs of revived distributive bargaining in Latin America.

The Ghana collaboration deepened relations between the international and the company. The efficiency of company investments was raised by union involvement under the general education umbrella: awareness raising, peer counselling and workplace representative education. The results for workers were also considerable, raising participation rates in the company's HIV/AIDS programmes while minimising risks to individuals. In Colombia, serious political factionalism within unions in an endemically violent situation was overcome and the GUF rebuilt dialogue with AA and other companies. Education was used in different ways in Africa and Latin America. In Africa, it was a mix of peer counsellor and workplace representative education while in Latin America it took more 'classical' forms beginning with representative education, and subsequently shifting to discussion of union structures and ways of working. In both contexts education was a major factor in building relationships, local capacity and creating the possibility of dialogue with AA. The case shows the significance of educational work and, in its African dimension, of the usefulness of a minilateral approach to it.

The ICEM was a major actor in its own right in the two continents that are central to AA's mining operations, taking initiative and mediating between the company and national unions. The formal collective bargaining that resulted in an IFA with Anglo Gold played a relatively minor role here. The GUF's input was important in taking the initiative with the AA companies and in negotiating significant safeguards for workers, in educating them and their representatives and in generalising and publicising the initiative beyond the company. A model was developed that the GUF transferred elsewhere in the world.

The case illustrates the large-scale resources required to form and maintain a relationship between a GUF and a multinational, as well as the potential rewards for doing so. The resources issue is one factor prompting us to ask how far lessons from the case can have wider significance, since GUFs have limited capacities to conduct such intensive long-term work. We can only broadly estimate the case's wider significance here and a need exists for more case studies. In this instance, a partnership approach was possible because of the HIV/AIDS issue, which generated an exceptionally powerful business case for working with the GUF. Nevertheless, broadly similar health conditions exist and concern both mining and other companies (Gaunt, 2007). Moreover, the multinational was predisposed to regard engagement with the GUF positively since it was reconciled to trade unionism, was operating profitably, was accustomed to initiating collaboration with unions to reduce costs, and senior management shared industrial relations experience with the ICEM leadership. These may be unusual features, but they are clearly not unique since the company's federal structure, concern with CSR and raising efficiency through cost reduction are shared by many others.

As we remarked above, the study illustrates the scale of the resources required to achieve success in constructing relationships of this type, a subject central to the next, concluding chapter.

III
Conclusion

CHAPTER NINE

The Political Decision

THE internationals currently face a remarkable situation. On the one hand they are politically unified, have high membership, and good levels of engagement with unions. For the first time in history, they can realistically claim to approximate to being genuinely global bodies. On the other hand, they are victims of their own success in bringing in more affiliates since demands increase as resources diminish, and completion of the globalisation process will intensify the problem. There are two competing logics at work: those of legitimacy and resources. The logic of legitimacy demands that new, unaffiliated unions and groups of currently unorganised workers are recruited. The logic of resources is that integrating these into the internationals will simply deepen the financial crisis.

Without functioning internationals, supported intelligently by their affiliates, the majority of the world's trade unions have weak relationships and leverage with employers. The extremely high level of international connectedness needed to develop this leverage cannot be established through bilateral contacts. Some have been tempted opportunistically to adopt the single-track 'rank and file internationalism is what counts' line to justify the development of bilateral links rather than to sustain and develop the internationals. But bilateralism fails to address the underlying power dynamics both between unions, and between unions and employers. Bilateral contacts are established, managed and funded only by a select group of unions in rich, developed countries, and as a result are likely to reinforce existing power imbalances. For successful internationalism to be built, these power disparities have to be overcome.

Power disparities are lived out through the issue of resources. There is no alternative to increasing the resources flowing from national to international level if the internationals are to survive, and more will be required to develop in the directions we suggest. If unions do not make the necessary financial commitment, the only alternative for the internationals and their affiliates is to become even more dependent on a small group of donors for projects that they may well be unable or unwilling to fund, or to become more reliant on employers who will exact a toll. This dependency on external funds is already, as we showed earlier, at a dangerously high level. Yet in a few cases unions have reduced or even ended their international subscriptions; many others simply affiliate small numbers of members or delay paying their dues. It is understandable that unions who are hard pressed and having difficulties in assisting their members should look to economise by restricting their payments to the internationals, but it is also a real issue in the era of globalisation.

The resources debate is becoming more public and is surfacing in conferences rather than behind closed doors. This leaves us with, at best, opportunities to make the political argument to union membership and executives to reinforce their international commitments. The transfer of resources from relatively prosperous nations' unions to others needs to be argued for at the political level not solely as an act of solidarity, nor as a form of protection against 'social dumping', but as an investment in their futures. A unionism is assumed here that sees all unions as interconnected workers' organisations, the demise of which in any country weakens the position of unions everywhere.

Which area of work should the internationals prioritise? They have three overlapping but distinct functions. First, they defend the existing space in which unions operate. Second, they work to create further space. Third, they help unions build the capacities to exploit that space, by helping unions to carry out core and new tasks more effectively. This last function is mainly carried out through the internationals' educational work. We stress that we do not argue here for the abandonment of any specific area of activity, all of which are relevant. Rather, a shift in the balance between these areas of activity is recommended, with an even greater emphasis being placed on education.

The first function, defending space, would be difficult to abandon or devolve, and not simply because of the importance to trade unionists of the duty of solidarity. The increasing worldwide tendency for the freedom of association to be attacked is a serious issue. The internationals have a unique status as institutions that unions can draw on when defending victimised activists at national level, which no national union can replicate. For the ITUC, with a formal status within the ILO governing body, this is especially relevant and the ITUC should continue to be concerned with human rights complaints mechanisms and continue to act as the political voice of international labour. Despite small results to date, political lobbying is an important area, one in which the ITUC should come into its own. The real prize is the creation of a social clause in World Trade Organisation proceedings, by linking trade with labour standards (Ewing and Sibley, 2000). As these authors point out, there are 'serious political and practical problems to be overcome' (*ibid.*: 39–40), but such a clause would open many possibilities for unions at national level, improving the possibilities for applying basic trade union rights and core labour standards throughout corporate structures and supply chains. The ITUC has the relevant expertise, tradition and track record in such lobbying work. The GUFs would obviously retain some of their role in complaints by virtue of their role in monitoring IFAs and specific rights abuses with employers, but our suggestion is for as much of this work as possible to be devolved to the umbrella body.

The second function, creating space, mainly but not exclusively through negotiating International Framework Agreements, should remain a significant area of GUF activity since it clearly provides opportunities for unions at local level. The way that these agreements should be conceptualised and presented to companies should perhaps be that adopted by the IUF, i.e. as recognition agreements rather than the more abstract framework agreements. Furthermore, they require support by improved company networking that, as we have argued, requires a more long-term educational approach. However, these agreements' limitations are thrown into sharp relief by the externalisation of much multinational employment and the explosion of 'informal' work, realities that appear unlikely to change greatly in the near future.

This area of work could also to some extent be devolved to different actors. Negotiation is not currently a core competence of the internationals, since many of their employees have relatively little in-depth experience of it. National unions, especially those in Europe, have more expertise, but devolution to them carries a significant risk. This has already been underlined, i.e. that some affiliates in the developed world may use it as an opportunity to further reinforce their prominent position in companies. Companies might try to create more space for themselves by exploiting the increased role it gives headquarters unions. This shift, therefore, would have to be carefully structured, policed and managed by GUFs. It might also be possible in some circumstances to devolve the monitoring of IFAs to a new institution that brought together the ILO, consultants and national unions, including those outside the OECD countries.

The third function, helping unions to exploit space, is a major candidate for expansion. Education is important to all levels of union activity, from organising informal workers to international networking. Moreover, imbalances in democratic participation may be addressed by the same means. Both unions and the internationals themselves stand to benefit greatly from such an increase in participation in their representative structures. As others have suggested (see, for example, Hannigan, 1998), the trade union movement would find labour educators only too willing to act with them to create an effective alliance.

There is an evident need for unions to rethink and reposition themselves, both in relation to their national contexts and employers – that is, to carry out transformational change. This has been particularly evident in the case of unions from the former Soviet Union and will be similarly significant in the Middle East and China. By 'transformational change' we mean involving members, aligning unions' structures with their missions and reallocating resources (Behrens et al., 2004). Education is of major importance in this profound type of change. In this context, it has two main aims. The first is to help unions to build their capacities to organise and mobilise workers. The second aim is to aid the union's organisational development. Organisational development supports organising in that it encourages unions to provide the necessary human resources, information and institutional support to carry it out. Such a perspective is at least a medium-term one and, for some unions, it will take a sustained and determined effort to achieve tangible results. If experience of organising approaches in the developed world teaches us anything, it is that there are no quick fixes.

Education should clearly be adapted to the needs in particular regions. More importantly, it should be linked directly to specific forms of experimentation considered particularly relevant by the unions concerned. Thus, it might focus on organising approaches, on the recruitment of particular types of worker or on mobilising and working with those already recruited. This type of approach is likely to appeal to the many unions in the world faced by large numbers of informal workers. As argued in Chapter seven from experience of precisely these kinds of programmes, efforts should be directed towards local, inter- and intra-regional groups of national unions exchanging experience, allowing unions to pool experience about what works best and under what circumstances. This would also allow unions to tap into those creative possibilities offered by local successes in organising in certain parts of the world.

A precondition for this approach is that unions are selected for their commitment and capacity to carry out and sustain a programme of development. These unions could then act as national models for others to evaluate. There are two further conditions for success: first, that it is carried out by people with the requisite expertise in international union development, and second that it is fully integrated both into the work of the unions involved and that of the GUF itself.

A shift of responsibilities within the internationals as outlined above could provide resources for the educational bias that is required. This could be further assisted both by regions and groupings of countries within them, especially since regions play a key role in securing dues payments from affiliates. Although increased contributions from national unions are urgently needed, this will require time to deliver and, in the interim, it will be necessary to raise funds. Regions should help in terms of fundraising from union-sympathetic governments such as those of Brazil and South Africa, both of which have extensive funds that unions could bid for. It may be that in the future local and regional organisations are more able to access funding than their international secretariats. HIV/AIDS funding, for example, operates on a completely decentralised basis. Raising the level of active fund raising in the regions would help to address the balance of power within the internationals by providing the sub-regions and regions with more independent resources (Wedin, 1991). The democratising effects of education should help to ensure that these funds are used in accountable ways.

In short, we find the emphasis developed by Levinson and adopted by many in the international union movement today on collective bargaining as a key task for GUFs to be misplaced. Instead, particularly given the profound informalisation of work that is taking place, unions need to focus their resources on using education and exchange of experience between trade unionists to maintain their relevance and legitimacy as the voice of labour.

The key remaining question is how to develop structures that take serious account of the importance of unions being able to articulate their experience and political work to their counterparts in other countries. The 'problem of large numbers' (see Chapter four) is a significant block to the level of cooperation and solidarity both within and between unions. As Olson argued: 'The larger the group, the less it will further its common interest' (Olson, 1965: 36).

Small groups operating within a multilateral structure provide the best method of articulation between trade union memberships, GUF affiliates and global unions. Our proposed way of working stimulates a closeness that the majority of the internationals' passive membership rarely experiences. Working in small groups provides a way of making multilateralism function because these groups can build on affiliates' proximity and serve to facilitate exchanges and transfers of capacity between them. The shared principles of the multilateral structures provide the necessary sense of inclusion and common purpose in a wider enterprise to the small groups. Cooperation within and between small groups is also relevant to the relationships between the GUFs themselves. It is an approach that the GUFs have recently adopted in a piecemeal fashion, but collaboration on issues of strategic importance should become a major focus in the future.

We have tried here to bring the current state of international trade unionism, a largely neglected dimension of globalisation, to the attention of a wider audience. The internationals' fragility and dependence on external resources is a problem that can only be overcome by a range of measures, including a higher level of commitment by unions in the developed world, particularly those from Europe, North America and Japan. The challenge to national unions is to contribute more to the internationals in order to secure their survival, an issue that has to be addressed with some urgency.

Simply put, the internationals' affiliates need to make the difficult but crucial political decision to support them with the resources they need. The global unions are the only institutions that can develop the collective experience, articulation and collaboration between unions in the ways demanded by globalisation.

Annex 1: BWI Model IFA

BWI Model International Framework Agreement

Approved by BWI World Council on 16 November 2007
Building and Wood Workers' International

To be signed between (company name) and the Building and Wood Workers' International (BWI) to promote and protect worker's rights.

A paragraph(s) should be inserted at the beginning of the agreement giving a short description of the company and its operations. ("The company recognises that corruption, bribery and unfair anti-competitive actions distort markets and hamper economic, social and democratic development." Should be part of the policy statement.)

The BWI is the Global Union Federation grouping free and democratic unions with members in the Building, Building Materials, Wood, Forestry and Allied sectors. The BWI groups together around 350 trade unions representing around 12 million members in 135 countries. The BWI's mission is to promote the development of trade unions in the building and wood industries throughout the world and to promote and enforce workers' rights.

The agreement is based on the signatories' joint commitment to respect basic human and trade union rights, acknowledging the fundamental principals of human rights as defined in the Universal Declaration of Human Rights, the ILO Declaration on Fundamental Principles and Rights at Work as well as relevant ILO Conventions and jurisprudence and the OECD guidelines on Multinational Companies. The parties also commit themselves to achieving continuous improvements within the areas of working conditions, health and safety standards at the workplace and positive democratic industrial relations and fair collective bargaining procedures with representative trade unions.

This agreement relates to all (company name) operations. The (company name) will secure compliance with the principles set out in this agreement also with its subsidiaries, contractors, subcontractors, suppliers and joint ventures. This agreement shall not in any way reduce or undermine existing labour relations practices or agreements relating to union rights or facilities already established by any BWI affiliate or group of affiliates or any other union within (company name).

In this spirit the (company name) and the BWI shall work together to verify the effective application by all (company name) activities and undertakings of the following requirements.

1. Freedom of association and the right to collective bargaining are respected

All workers shall have the right to form and join trade unions of their own choice. These unions shall have the right to be recognised for the purpose of collective bargaining in conformance with ILO Conventions 87 and 98. Workers' representatives shall not be subjected to any discrimination and shall have access to all necessary workplaces in order to carry out their duties as representatives (ILO Convention 135 and Recommendation 143). The company shall take a positive attitude to trade union activities, including union access to workers in the organising process. The company will follow the most efficient process in the event that BWI affiliate requests union recognition.

2. Employment is freely chosen

There shall be no use of forced or compulsory labour, including bonded labour. Workers shall not be asked to surrender passports, identity papers or valuables (ILO Conventions 29 and 105).

3. No discrimination in employment

All workers shall have equality of opportunity and treatment regardless of their ethnic origin, gender, religion, political opinion, nationality, social origin or other distinguishing characteristics. Workers shall receive equal pay for work of equal value (ILO Conventions 100 and 111). Migrating and posted employees must enjoy at least the same conditions as the national work force.

4. Child labour is not used

Child labour shall not be used. Only workers above the age of 15 years, or over the compulsory school-leaving age if higher, shall be employed (ILO Convention 138). Children under the age of 18 shall not perform work which, by its nature or the circumstances in which it is carried out, is likely to harm the health, safety or morals of children (ILO Convention 182).

5. Living wages are paid

Workers shall be paid wages and benefits for a standard working week that will enable them and their families to enjoy a reasonable standard of living, and which are more favourable than the minimum conditions established by national legislation or agreements. All workers must be provided with clear verbal and written information about wage conditions, as well as specific information regarding every payment period (ILO Conventions 131 Minimum Wage Fixing, 1970, C.95 Protection of wages, 1949, C.94 Labour Clauses (Public Contracts), 1949). Deductions shall not be made from wages unless otherwise stated in national law or collective agreements. Information regarding pay and deductions should be provided to workers each time wages are paid, and these should not be changed other than by written consent of the individual worker or by collective agreement.

6. Hours of work are not excessive

Hours of work shall comply with appropriate national legislation, national agreements and industry standards but in no circumstances should be unreasonable. Overtime shall not be excessive, shall not be demanded on a regular basis and shall always be remunerated at a premium rate. All workers shall be given a minimum of a one day weekly rest period.

7. Health and Safety of Workers

A safe and healthy working environment shall be provided. Best occupational health and safety practice to prevent injuries and ill health shall be promoted and shall be in compliance with ILO Convention 155 Occupational Safety and Health Convention, 1981 and ILO Convention 167 on Safety and Health in Construction, 1988 and the ILO Guidelines for Occupational Health Management Systems.

All workers shall also be given Personal Protective Equipment, at no cost to themselves, and training on occupational hazards and their prevention. Workplace Health and Safety Committees shall be established and workers shall have the right to elect Health and Safety Representatives. Trade Unions shall be encouraged to appoint and train Health and Safety Representatives.

Suppliers, contractors and sub-contractors shall be required to provide a site-specific health and safety plan and to appoint a competent person to manage health and safety and to take part in safety meetings.

8. Welfare of workers

At every work site the company shall provide an adequate supply of wholesome drinking water; sanitary and washing facilities; facilities for changing and for storage and drying of clothing; accommodation for taking meals and for shelter.

When workers are offered living accommodation, this shall be planned, built and maintained to provide reasonable housing conditions. The company shall provide health education and an HIV/AIDS awareness raising and prevention programme in accordance with the ILO Code of Practice on HIV/AIDS and the World of Work.

9. Skills training

All workers shall have the opportunity to participate in education and training programmes including training to improve workers skills to use new technology and equipment.

10. The employment relationship is established

The company shall respect obligations to all workers under labour and social security laws and regulations arising from the regular employment relationship (Social Security Minimum Standards Convention C.102). In locations where conditions permit, efforts shall be made to offer fixed employment opportunities. All workers shall receive a written contract of employment. The company and all sub-contractors shall, wherever practicable, directly employ all labour, and shall pay social security and pension contributions for their workers.

IMPLEMENTATION

The (company name) will ensure that appropriate translations of the agreement are available at all workplaces and should include suppliers and subcontractors. The agreement will also be made public on the Company's website and Intranet.

a) Both parties recognize that effective local monitoring of this agreement must involve the local management, the workers and their representatives, health and safety representatives and local trade unions.

b) To enable local and national union representatives of BWI affiliated unions to play a role in the monitoring process, they will be given adequate time for training and involvement in the monitoring process. The company will ensure that they are provided with information, access to workers, and rights of inspection necessary to effectively monitor compliance with this agreement.

c) A reference group shall be set up, composed of representatives of (Company name), and of the concerned BWI affiliated union(s) in the home country of the company and a BWI coordinator. It will meet at least once a year, or when necessary, to evaluate reports on compliance and to review the implementation of the agreement.

(company name) shall make the necessary resources available for the implementation of the agreement.

Trade union representation should be secured in internal or external monitoring. Monitoring or audit reports should be made available to the signing organisations.

The annual review of the present agreement shall be incorporated into (company name) annual reporting with the consent of the signatories.

CONFLICT RESOLUTION

In the event of a complaint or an infraction of the agreement the following procedure will normally apply:

a) Firstly, the complaint should be raised with the local site management.

b) If the complaint is not resolved with local management, it should be referred to the appropriate national union who will raise the issue with the company.

c) Any infractions which could not be resolved through discussion at the workplace or national level will be addressed by the BWI coordinator in close cooperation with the BWI affiliates in the home country and will be reported to the responsible manager, who will ensure that corrective measures are implemented in a timely manner.

d) If the issue is not resolved, the reference group will deal with the matter and propose appropriate action.

e) If corrective measures are not taken in a way that is satisfactory to the BWI affiliate raising the complaint, and the BWI-affiliate and the BWI coordinator participating in the reference group, the dispute shall be resolved through binding arbitration. The arbitrator will be jointly selected by all of the members of the reference group. All expenses for the arbitration will be the responsibility of the Company.

f) If a dispute is not resolved and breaches continue, withdrawal from the IFA should be a final resort.

Signatories agree that any difference arising from the interpretation or implementation of this agreement will be examined jointly, for the purpose of clarification.

DURATION

This agreement is effective from today's date, with a mutual three month notice of termination.

Date and venue

(Signature Building and Wood Workers' International, BWI)

&

(Signature company name)

Annex 2: Lafarge IFA

Agreement on corporate social responsibility and international industrial relations signed between the Lafarge Group and the International trade union federations IFBWW, ICEM and WFBW to promote and protect workers' rights

The IFBWW, International Federation of Building and Wood Workers, is a Global Union Federation organising more than 10.5 million members in 281 trade unions in 125 countries around the world in the building, building materials, wood, forestry and allied industries.

The ICEM, International Federation of Chemical, Energy, Mine and General Workers' Unions, is a Global Union Federation organising workers in the Chemical, Energy, Mine and related Process Industries including Cement, Glass and Ceramics. ICEM unites 425 member trade unions from 121 countries representing in total around 20 million workers in these industries.

The WFBW, World Federation of Building and Woodworkers' Unions, represents 1.5 million workers in the building and wood industry and who are organised in 55 unions in 41 countries all over the world.

Lafarge is the world leader in building materials, holds top-ranking positions in all four of its Divisions: Cement, Aggregates & Concrete, Roofing and Gypsum. Lafarge employs 77,000 people in 75 countries.

PREAMBLE

Lafarge believes that there's a link between social and economic progress. The interests and success of Lafarge and its employees are interdependent. Lafarge commits itself to involve its employees directly in the Group future through an open dialog; Lafarge recognizes that employees may choose to be represented by elected employees and/or trade union organizations.

The Lafarge philosophy is to develop and maintain positive relationships with its employees in accordance with the 'Lafarge Principles of Action': "Lafarge responsibility is as much about complying with local and international laws and standards as it is about aligning our actions with our values. Respect for the common interest, openness and dialog, integrity and commitment are the main ethical principles of the Group and of the employees".

Trade unions believe that decent wages and working conditions, a meaningful job with prospects, a safe and healthy working environment, the right to join free trade unions and the right to collective bargaining are preconditions for good industrial relations.

The signatories consider that this agreement is based on the joint commitment to respect human and social rights and to achieve continuous improvement within the areas of working conditions, industrial relations, health and safety standards in the workplace and environmental performance.

The signatories recognize that the subsidiarity principle is a key performance management process within the Group; therefore the signatories respect the principle that industrial relations issues are best resolved as close as possible to the workplaces.

Lafarge considers respect for workers' rights to be a crucial element in sustainable development. Lafarge will seek to use the services of those trading partners, subcontractors and suppliers, which recognise and implement the principles listed below.

FUNDAMENTAL PRINCIPLES

Lafarge commits itself to comply with the International Labour Organization (ILO) Declaration on Fundamental Principles and Rights at Work, the ILO Tripartite Declaration of Principles concerning Multinational Enterprises and Social Policy, the United Nations Global Compact and also the Organisation for Economic Cooperation and Development Guidelines for Multinational Enterprises.

No forced labour

It is prohibited to make direct or indirect use of forced labour, including bonded labour and involuntary prison labour (ILO Conventions 29 and 105).

No discrimination in employment

All workers, whatever their workplace, shall have equality of opportunity and treatment regardless of their ethnic origin, colour, gender, religion, political opinion, nationality, social origin or other distinguishing characteristics. Workers shall receive equal pay for work of equal value (ILO Conventions 100 and 111). Migrant and posted employees must be ensured at least the same rights and conditions as the national workforce working in the company.

No use of child labour

It is prohibited to use child labour in any form whatsoever: only workers above the age of 15 years, or over the compulsory school-leaving age if higher, shall be employed (ILO Convention 138). In view of their age, children under the age of 18 shall not perform work, which, by its nature or the circumstances in which it is carried out, is likely to harm the health, safety or morals of children (ILO Convention 182).

Freedom of association and right to collective bargaining

Lafarge should uphold the freedom of association and the effective recognition of the right to collective bargaining (ILO conventions 87 and 98).

The Lafarge Group guarantees that workers' representatives shall not be discriminated against (ILO Convention 135).

Living wages

Workers shall be paid wages and benefits for a standard working week that should be at least at the level of current national legislation or collective agreements, as applied in the industry/sector concerned. All workers must be provided with clear verbal and written information about wage conditions in their native language.

Deductions from wages, unless permitted under national law, shall not be made under any circumstances without the express permission of the worker concerned.

Working hours

Working hours shall comply with appropriate national legislation, national agreements and industry/sector standards. Overtime shall not be excessive and shall always be remunerated at a premium rate. All workers shall be given a minimum of a one day weekly rest period.

Health, safety and working conditions

A safe and healthy working environment shall be provided (ILO Convention 155). Best occupational health and safety practices shall be followed and shall be in compliance with the ILO Guidelines for Occupational Health Management Systems. All workers shall be given training on occupational hazards and shall have the means of preventing them.

The signatories undertake to raise awareness of the HIV/AIDS problem and of the prevention programme in compliance with the ILO HIV/AIDS code of practice.

Skills training

All workers shall have the opportunity to participate in education and training programmes including training to improve workers' level of skills so that they can use new technology and equipment. Whenever possible, the Lafarge Group in cooperation with trade unions shall develop workers' training with a view to improving their level of skills and ensuring that they participate in their career development and increase their employability.

IMPLEMENTATION AND FOLLOW UP

The Lafarge Group will provide information concerning this agreement in written or verbal form in all countries where this agreement is applicable.

All signatories are strongly committed to the most widespread dissemination possible of the content of this agreement throughout the Lafarge operations.

A reference group consisting of representatives of the Lafarge management and the signatory international federations shall meet at least once a year, or whenever necessary, to follow up and review the implementation of this agreement.

The Lafarge Group shall make available to the reference group the resources needed for its mission.

The annual review of the present agreement should be incorporated into the Lafarge Group's reporting with the consent of all signatories.

All signatories agree that any difference arising from the interpretation or implementation of this agreement will be examined jointly, for the purpose of making recommendations to the signatories concerned.

DURATION

This agreement shall remain in force unless otherwise agreed by any party giving three calendar month's notice, in writing, to the other.

The present agreement may be revised at the request of one of the signatories no later than four years after it has been signed.

Paris, 12 September 2005

The Lafarge Group, Christian Herrault
The IFBWW, Anita Normark
The ICEM, Fred Higgs
The WFBW, Stefaan Vantourenhout

References

Abott, J. (1997) 'Export processing zones and the developing world', *Contemporary Review*, May: 1–4.

Ananaba, W. (1979) *The Trade Union Movement in Africa: Promise and performance*. London: Hurst.

Andersson, U., Forsoren, M. and Holm, U. (2007) 'Balancing subsidiary influence in a federative MNC: a business network view', *Journal of International Business Studies*, 38: 802–18.

Anglo American (2003) Tony Traher's speech to the AGM, 28 March.

_____ (2007) *Response to allegations made in War on Want's 'Anglo American—the alternative report' 2007*. London: Anglo American.

_____ (2008) Sir Mark Moody-Stuart's speech to the AGM, 12 March.

Anner, M., Greer, I., Hauptmeier, M., Lillie, N. and Winchester, N. (2006) 'The industrial determinants of transnational solidarity: Global interunion politics in three sectors', *European Journal of Industrial Relations*, 12 (1): 7–27.

Anyemedu, K. (2000) *Trade union responses to globalization: Case study on Ghana*. Geneva: ILO: Institute of Employment Studies.

Archer, C. (2001) *International Organizations*. London: Routledge.

Axelrod, R. and Keohane, R.O. (1986) 'Achieving cooperation under anarchy: strategies and institutions', in Oye, K. (ed.), *Cooperation under Anarchy*. Princeton University Press.

Bales, K. (2004) *Disposable People: New slavery in the global economy*. Berkeley CA: University of California Press.

Barrientos, S. (2002) 'Mapping codes through the value chain: from researcher to detective', in Jenkins, R., Pearson, R. and Seyfang, G., *Corporate Responsibility and Labour Rights: Codes of Conduct in the Global Economy*. London: Earthscan: 61–78.

Batliwala, S. (2002) 'Grassroots movements as transnational actors: implications for global civil society', *Voluntas*, 13 (4): 393–409.

Bécu, O. (1966) 'Vorwort', in Gottfurcht, H., *Die Internationale Gewerkschaftsbewegung von den Anfang bis zur Gegenwart*. Köln: Bund Verlag: 5–6.

Behrens, M., Hurd, R. and Waddington, J. (2004) 'How does union restructuring contribute to union revitalization?', in Frege, C.M. and Kelly, J. (eds), *Varieties of Unionism*. Oxford: Oxford University Press: 11–30.

Beirnaert, J. (2008) 'A problem that transcends all boundaries', *International Union Rights*, 14 (4): 3–4.

Bendiner, B. (1987) *International Labour Affairs: the world trade unions and the multinational companies*. Oxford: Clarendon Press.

Berger, P.L. and Godsell, B. (1988) *A Future South Africa: visions, strategies and realities*. London: Westview Press.

Bidoli, M. (2004) 'Beyond the bottom line', *Financial Mail* (South Africa), 7 May.

Blowfield, M. and Frynas, J.G. (2005) 'Setting new agendas: Critical perspectives on CSR in the Developing World', *International Affairs*, 81 (3): 499–513.

Blyth, A. (2003) 'Corporate responsibility at Danone', *Ethical Business*, 17 December.

Bognanno, M.F., Keane, M.P. and Yang, D. (2005) 'The influence of wages and industrial relations environments on the production location decisions of US Multi National Corporations', *Industrial and Labor Relations Review*, 58: 171–200.

Bonner, C. (2006) *Organising informal transport workers: Global Research project*. London: ITF.

Buckley, P.J. (2000) *Multinational firms, cooperation and competition in the world economy*. Basingstoke: Macmillan.

Bundesinstitut für Arbeit (1993 and 2007) *Arbeitnehmerüberlassungssatistik*. Berlin: BfA.

Burke, L. (1996) 'How Corporate Social Responsibility pays off', *Long Range Planning*, 29: 495–502.

Busch, G.K. (1983) *The political role of international trades unions*. London: Macmillan Press.

Buschak, W. (2002) *Edo Fimmen: Der schöne Traum von Europa und die Globalisierung. Eine Biografie*. Essen: Klartext Verlag.

_____ (2003) 'The European Trade Union Confederation and the European Industry Federations', in FES, *European Trade Union Organisations: Inventory of the Archive of Social Democracy and the Archive of the Friedrich Ebert Stiftung*. Bonn: published on behalf of the FES by Optenhögel, U., Schneider, M. and Zimmerman, R.: 9–19.

Business Action in Africa (2007) *Business and HIV/AIDS: what we have learnt*. London: Business Action in Africa.

BWI (2004) *BWI experiences with Global Company Agreement*. Brussels: BWI. European Industrial Relations Observatory On Line.

Caldwell, P. (1998) 'Labour Education and New Unionism in the UK: The Case of UNISON'. Paper to UCLA/AFL-CIO Education Conference, Los Angeles, 30 April – 2 May.

Carew, A. (1987) *Labour Under the Marshall Plan: the politics of productivity and the marketing of management science*. Manchester: Manchester University Press.

_____ (2000) 'Towards a free trade union centre: The International Confederation of Free Trade Unions (1949–1972)', in Carew, A., Dreyfus, M., Van Goethem, G., Gumbrell-McCormick, R. and van der Linden, M. (eds), *The International Confederation of Free Trade Unions*. Berne: Peter Lang: 187–337.

_____ (2007) 'The Trades Union Congress in the international labour movement', in

Campbell, A., Fishman, N. and McIlroy, J., *The Post-War compromise: British trade unions and industrial politics 1945–64*. Monmouth: Merlin Press: 145–67.

Carling, A. (ed.) (2006) *Globalization and Identity*. London: I.B. Tauris.

Chaison, G. (1996) *Union Mergers in Hard Times*. Ithaca NY: Cornell University Press.

Charoenloet, V., Ativanichayapong, N. and Wanabriboon, P. (2004) *The Impact of Trade Union Solidarity Support Organisations in Thailand 1993–2002*. Bonn: Friedrich Ebert Stiftung.

Chen, M.A. (2007) *Re-thinking the informal economy: linkages with the formal economy and the formal regulatory environment*. New York: United Nations Department for Economic and Social Affairs, working paper 46.

CISL [Confédération international des syndicats libres] (1972) *La fonction syndicale au course des années 70*. Brussels: CISL.

Clark, P.F., Gilbert, K., Gray, L.S. and Solomon, N. (1998) *Union administrative practices: a comparative analysis*. Ithaca NY: DigitalCommons@ILR, Cornell University.

Clarke, S. (2007) 'The State of the Russian Unions', *Journal of Labor Research*, 18 (2): 275–99.

Collins, H. and Abramsky, C. (1965) *Karl Marx and the British Labour Movement: Years of the First International*. London: Macmillan.

Cooke, W.N. (1997) 'The influence of industrial relations factors on US direct investment abroad', *Industrial and Labor Relations Review*, 51: 3–17.

Croucher, R. (2003) 'African Labour', *Historical Studies in Industrial Relations*, 13: 95–112.

_____ (2004) 'The impact of trade union education: a study from three countries in Eastern Europe', *European Journal of Industrial Relations*, 10 (1): 90–109.

Croucher, R. and Halstead, J. (1990) 'The origin of "Liberal" adult education for miners at Sheffield in the post-war period: A study in adult education and the working class', *Trade Union Studies Journal*, 21: 3–14.

Croucher, R. and Singe, I. (2004) 'Co-determination and working time accounts in the German finance industry', *Industrial Relations Journal*, 35 (2):153–68.

Croucher, R., Tyson, S. and Wild, A. (2006) '"Peak" Employers' Organisations: International attempts at transferring experience', *Economic and Industrial Democracy*, 27 (3): 469–90.

Dempsey, M. (2004) *Managing trade unions. A case study examination of managerial activities in four UK trade unions formed by merger*. Unpublished PhD thesis, Cranfield University.

Dølvik, J.E. (1997) 'EWCs and the implications for Europeanisation of collective bargaining', in Dølvik, J.E. (ed.), *Re-drawing the boundaries of solidarity? ETUC, social dialogue and the Europeanisation of trade unions in the 1990s*. Oslo: Arena/FAFO: 381–91.

Douzinas, C. (2000) *The End of Human Rights*. Oxford: Hart Publishing.

Dreyfus, M. (2000) 'The emergence of an international trade union organization', in Carew, A., Dreyfus, M., Van Goethem, G., Gumbrell-McCormick, R. and van der Linden, M. (eds), *The International Confederation of Free Trade Unions*. Berne: Peter Lang: 25–68.

Eder, M. (2002) 'The constraints on labour internationalism', in Harrod, J. and O'Brien, R. (eds), *Global Unions? Theory and strategies of organized labour in the global political economy*. London: Routledge: 167–84.

Edwards, M. (2001) *NGO Rights and Responsibilities: a new deal for global governance*. London: Foreign Policy Centre.

Elliott, K.A. and Freeman, R.B. (2003) *Can Labor Standards Improve Under Globalization?* Washington: Institute for International Economics.

Erne, R. (2006) 'European trade union strategies: between technocratic efficiency and democratic legitimacy', in Smisman, S. (ed.), *Civil Society and Legitimate European Governance*. Cheltenham: Edward Elgar: 219–40.

_____ (2008) *European Unions: Labor's quest for a transnational democracy*. Ithaca NY: Cornell University Press.

European Foundation for the Improvement of Living and Working Conditions (2003) EWC Case Study: Daimler Chrysler Group. http://www.eurofound.europa.eu/areas/participationatwork/ewccasestudies.htm (Accessed 15 August 2008).

Ewing, K.D. and Sibley, T. (2000) *International Trade Union Rights for the New Millennium*. London: Institute of Employment Rights.

Fairbrother, P. and Hammer, N. (2005) 'Global unions: Past efforts and future prospects', *Relations Industrielles/Industrial Relations*, 60 (3): 405–31.

Fairbrother, P., Williams, G., Barton, R.R., Gibellieri, E. and Tropeoli, A. (2007) 'Unions facing the future: Questions and possibilities', *Labour Studies Journal*, 31 (4): 31–53.

Feidel-Mertz, H. (1964) *Zur Ideologie der Arbeiterbildung*. Frankfurt: EVA.

Fenton O'Creevy, M., Cerdin, J.-C. and Gooderham, P. (2007) 'Lost in translation? Developing the skills of knowledge-sharing within multinational corporations' Symposium paper, 'the development of social capital for knowledge-sharing purposes in MNCs' Academy of Management Conference, Philadelphia, 6 August.

Fichter, M. and Sydow, J. (2002) 'Using networks towards Global Labour Standards? Organising social responsibility in Global Production Chains', *Industrielle Beziehungen*, 9 (4): 357–80.

Fimmen, E. (1922) *The International Federation of Trade Unions: Its development and aims*. Publications of the International Federation of Trade Unions, 1.

_____ (1924) *Labour's Alternative: The United States of Europe or Europe Limited*. London: Labour Publishing Company.

Flanagan, R.J. (2006) 'Multinational corporations and labour conditions', *Globalization and labour conditions*. Oxford scholarship online monograph.

Frazer, G. (2008) 'Industrial Relations in Ghana', in Wood, G. and Brewster, C. (eds), *Industrial Relations in Africa*. Basingstoke: Palgrave: 182–97.

Freeman, R.B. and Medoff, J.L. (1984) *What Unions Do*. New York: Basic Books.

Freire, P. (1970) *The Pedagogy of the Oppressed*. New York: The Continuum Publishing Company.

Galbraith, J.K. (1983) *An Anatomy of Power*. New York: Houghton Mifflin.

Gallin, D. (1997) *Funeral oration for Charles Levinson, January 26, 1997.* Geneva: Global Labour Institute, www.global-labour.org.

Garver, P., Buketov, K., Chong, H. and Sosa Martinez, B. (2007) 'Global labor organizing in theory and practice', *Labour Studies Journal*, 32: 236–56.

Gaunt, R. (2007) *Making disease management pay.* London: International Council on mining and metals.

Gills, B.K. (2000) *Globalization and the Politics of Resistance.* New York: St Martin's Press.

Glyn, A. (2006) *Capitalism unleashed: Finance, globalization and welfare.* Oxford: Oxford University Press.

Gooderham, P., Nordhaug, O. and Ringdal, K. (1999) 'Institutional and Rational Determinants of Organizational Practices: Human Resource Management in European Firms', *Administrative Science Quarterly*, 44: 507–31.

_____ (2006) 'National Embeddedness and Calculative Human Resource Management in US Subsidiaries in Europe and Australia', *Human Relations*, 59 (11): 1,491–513.

Gottfurcht, H. (1962) *Die internationale Gewerkschaftsbewegung im Weltgeschehen: Geschichte, Probleme, Aufgaben.* Köln: Bund Verlag.

_____ (1966) *Die internationale Gewerkschaftsbewegung von den Anfängen bis zur Gegenwart.* Köln: Bund Verlag.

Graham, E.M. (2000) *Fighting the wrong enemy: Antiglobal activists and Multinational enterprises.* Washington DC: Institute for International Economics.

Greenfield, G. and Rossman, P. (2006) 'Financialization: New routes to profit, new challenges for trade unions', *Labour Education*, 2006/1, 142: 55–62.

Greenfield, G. (2006) 'The impact of financialization on transnational production systems: The role of new financial imperatives in the restructuring strategies of Nestlé, Kraft and Unilever'. Paper delivered to the International Workshop 'The impact of global production systems on trade union strategies', 10–11 May, Institute of Social Studies, The Hague, Netherlands.

Greven, T. (2003) 'Organische Solidarität und transnationale Kampagnen', in Croucher, R., Kruse, W., Martens, H., Singe, I. and Tech, D. (eds), *Transnationale Gewerkschaftskooperationen-Erfahrungen und Forschungsfragen.* Dortmund: Sozialforschungstelle: Beiträge aus der Forschung, Band 138: 92–104.

_____ (2006) 'US strategic campaigns against Trans National Enterprises in Germany', *Industrielle Beziehungen*, 13 (3): 1–17.

_____ (2008) 'United Steelworkers versus Continental AG: Transatlantic strategic campaigns', in Etges, A. (ed.), *Amerika und Europa.* Münster: Lit Verlag: 1–19.

Grindling, T.H. and Terrell, K. (2005) 'The effect of minimum wages on actual wages in formal and informal sectors in Costa Rica', *World Development*, 33 (11): 1,905–21.

Guliy, M. (2008) *Final project report on the Five GUFs project.* Moscow: IUF/ICEM/BWI/ITF/UNI.

Gumbrell-McCormick, R.A. (2000a) 'Facing New Challenges', in Carew, A., Dreyfus, M., Van Goethem, G., Gumbrell-McCormick, R.A. and van der Linden, M. (eds), *The*

International Confederation of Free Trade Unions. Berne: Peter Lang: 343–515.

_____ (2000b) 'Globalisme et Régionalisme', in Fouquet, A., Rehfeldt, U. and Le Roux, S. (eds), *Le Syndicalisme dans la Mondialisation.* Paris: les Editions de l'Atelier: 43–53.

_____ (2001) *The International Confederation of Free Trade Unions: structure, ideology and capacity to act.* Unpublished PhD Thesis, University of Warwick.

_____ (2002) *The ICFTU and Trade Unions in the Developing Countries: Solidarity or Dependence.* London: Birkbeck College, University of London.

_____ (2004) 'The ICFTU and the World Economy: A Historical Perspective', in Munck, R. (ed.), *Labour and Globalisation: Results and Prospects.* Liverpool: Liverpool University Press: 34–51.

Hagglund, G. (2007) 'The development of industrial relations in Kenya', in Wood, G. and Brewster, C., *Industrial Relations in Africa.* Basingstoke: Palgrave Macmillan: 28–38.

Hall, D. (2008) *Private Equity and employment: The Davos/WEF/Harvard study.* http://www.psiru.org (Accessed 15 August 2008).

Hammer, N. (2005) 'International Framework Agreements: global industrial relations between rights and bargaining', *Transfer,* 11 (4): 511–30.

Handley, A. (2005) 'Business, government and economic policy making in the new South Africa, 1990–2000', *Journal of Modern African Studies,* 43: 211–39.

Hannigan, T.A. (1998) *Managing Tomorrow's High-Performance Unions.* Westport CT: Quorum Books.

Harcourt, M., Wood, G. and Harcourt, S. (2004) 'Do unions affect employer compliance with the law?', *British Journal of Industrial Relations,* 42 (3): 527–41.

Herod, A. (2001) *Labor Geographies: workers and the landscapes of capitalism.* New York: Guildford Press.

Hirst, P. and Thompson, G. (2002) 'The future of globalization', *Co-operation and Conflict,* 37 (8): 247–65.

Hoffmann, A. (2005) *The construction of solidarity in a German Central Works Council: Implications for European Works Councils.* Unpublished PhD thesis, University of Warwick.

Hogan, M.J. (1989) *The Marshall Plan: America, Britain and the reconstruction of Western Europe.* Cambridge: Cambridge University Press.

Holdcroft, J. (2006) 'International Framework Agreements: A Progress Report', *Metalworld,* 3: 18–22.

Husted, B.W. (2003) 'Governance Choices for Corporate Social Responsibility: to contribute, collaborate or internalize', *Long Range Planning,* 36: 481–98.

Huzzard, T. (2000) *Labouring to learn: union renewal in Swedish manufacturing.* Umeå: Boréa.

Hyman, R. (2002) 'The international labour movement on the threshold of two centuries: Agitation, organisation, bureaucracy, diplomacy'. http://www.arbarkiv.nu/pdf_wri/Hyman_int.pdf (Accessed 15 August 2008).

ICEM (2003) 'Report of the Finance Sub Committee 2003'. Brussels: International

Federation of Chemical, Energy, Mine and General Workers' Unions.

_____ (2004a) *Contract/Agency Labour: A threat to our social standards*. Brussels: International Federation of Chemical, Energy, Mine and General Workers' Unions.

_____ (2004b) *Presidium Report 2004*. Brussels: International Federation of Chemical, Energy, Mine and General Workers' Unions.

_____ (2004c) *Finance and Restructuring Document 2004*. Brussels: International Federation of Chemical, Energy, Mine and General Workers' Unions.

ICFTU (1978) *The ICFTU Development Charter 1978*. Brussels: International Confederation of Free Trade Unions.

_____ (1990) *The Challenge of internationalization: a background document for the ICFTU/ITS Conference on Trade Unions and the Transnationals, 25–28 March 1990*. Elsinore, Denmark. Brussels: International Confederation of Free Trade Unions.

_____ (2000) *Report: 1ˢᵗ Meeting of the Progress Group September 2000*. Brussels: International Confederation of Free Trade Unions.

_____ (2001a) *Transforming the Global Economy: Report from the Global Economy Reference Group of the Millennium Project*. Brussels: International Confederation of Free Trade Unions.

_____ (2001b) *International Trade Union Strategies in Dealing with Companies and other Employers*. Brussels: International Confederation of Free Trade Unions.

_____ (2001c) *Report: 3ʳᵈ Meeting of the Millennium Review Progress Group*. Brussels: International Confederation of Free Trade Unions.

_____ (2001d) *Report of the Progress Group November 2001*. Brussels: International Confederation of Free Trade Unions.

_____ (2001e) *Background Report to the 117ᵗʰ meeting of the ICFTU Executive Board*. Brussels: International Confederation of Free Trade Unions.

_____ (2001f) *International Trade Union Organisation Resources and Services*. Brussels: International Confederation of Free Trade Unions.

_____ (2001g) *Strengthening National Trade Unions Research Paper*. Brussels: International Confederation of Free Trade Unions.

_____ (2001h) *The Future of the International Trade Union Movement*. Congress statement. Brussels: International Confederation of Free Trade Unions.

_____ (2003) *Export Processing Zones—symbols of exploitation and a development dead-end*. Brussels: International Confederation of Free Trade Unions.

_____ (2004) *Financial Reports*. Presented to the Eighteenth World Congress, Miyazaki, 5–10 December. Brussels: International Confederation of Free Trade Unions.

_____ (2006) *Fighting for Alternatives. Cases of successful trade union resistance to the policies of the International Monetary Fund and World Bank*. Brussels: International Confederation of Free Trade Unions in co-operation with the Global Union Research Network.

ILO (2003) *Information note on corporate social responsibility and international labour standards*. Geneva: ILO.

_____ (2007) *The Employment Relationship: an annotated guide to the ILO Recommendation 198*. Geneva: ILO.

IMF (1942) *Minutes of the IMF British Section Annual Meeting, 14 August*. MRC: MSS 36/ IMF/4. Geneva: IMF.

_____ (1944) *Minutes of IMF British Section Annual Meeting, 12 October*. MRC 159/1/16. Geneva: IMF.

_____ (2004) *Conclusions of the IMF World Auto Council Dearborn USA*. Geneva: IMF.

ITUC (2004) *ITUC 18th World Congress 2004: Report on Activities and Financial Reports*. Brussels: International Trade Union Confederation.

IUF (2007) *A Workers' Guide to Private Equity Buyouts*. Geneva: IUF.

Jones, G. (ed.) (1993) *Transnational Corporations: A historical perspective*. London: Routledge.

Kahler, M. (1992) 'Multilateralism with small and large numbers', *International Organization*, 46 (3): 681–708.

Kenny, B. (2004) 'The "Market Hegemonic" workplace order in food retailing', in Webster, E. and von Holdt, K. (eds), *Beyond the Apartheid Workplace: Studies in Transition*. Scottsville: University of Kwa Zulu Natal Press: 217–41.

Khaliy, I. (2005) *The effects of foreign-funded trade union education in Russia*. Moscow: Academy of Sciences.

Kirk, N. (2003) *Comrades and cousins: Globalization, workers and labour movements in Britain, the USA and Australia from the 1880s to 1914*. London: Merlin Press.

Kirton, G. and Healy, G. (2004) 'Shaping union and gender identities: a case study of women-only trade union courses', *British Journal of Industrial Relations*, 42 (2): 303–23.

Koch-Baumgarten, S. (1997) 'Spionage für Mitbestimmung: die Kooperation der Internationalen Transportarbeiterföderation mit allierten secret services im Zweiten Weltkrieg als korporatistiches Tauscharrangement', *Internationale Wissenschaftliche Korrespondenz zur Geschichte der deutschen Arbeiterbewegung*, 33: 361–90.

_____ (1998) 'Trade union regime formation under the conditions of globalization in the transport sector: attempts at transnational trade union regulation of flag-of-convenience shipping', *International Review of Social History*, 43 (3): 369–402.

Koftas, J.B. (2002) 'US foreign policy and the World Federation of Trade Unions, 1944–1948', *Diplomatic History*, 26 (1): 26–40.

Köhler, G. (2003) 'Foreign direct investment and its employment opportunities in perspective: meeting the great expectations of developing countries?', in Cooke, W.N. (ed.), *Multi-National Companies and Global Human Resource Strategies*. Westport CT: Greenwood Press: 21–42.

Köhnen, H. and Glaubitz, J. (2000) 'Wal-Mart: ein Wolf im Schafspelz?', *Die Mitbestimmung*, 6: 58–9.

Kratochwil, F. (1993) 'Norms versus numbers: multilateralism and the rationalist and reflexivist approaches to institutions – a unilateral plea for communicative rationality' in Ruggie, J. (ed.), *Multilateralism matters: The theory and praxis of an institutional form*. New York: Columbia University Press: 443–74.

Kristensen, P.H. and Zeitlin, J. (2005) *Local Players in Global Games: the Strategic Constitution of a Multinational Corporation*. Oxford: Oxford University Press.

Lecher, W., Platzer, H.-W., Fulton, L., Jaich, R., Rehfeldt, U., Rüb, S., Telljohann, V. and Weiner, K.P. (1999) *The establishment of European Works Councils: from information committee to social actor*. Aldershot: Ashgate.

Levinson, C. (1972) *International Trade Unionism*. Chicago IL: Aldine Publishing.

Lewis, H. (2003) *The International Transport Workers' Federation 1945–1965: An organizational and political anatomy*. Unpublished PhD thesis, University of Warwick.

Lieβ, O.R. (1983) 'Weltgewerkschaftsbund', in Mielke, S., *Internationales Gewerkschafts Handbuch*. Opladen: Leske und Budrich: 10–20.

Lillie, N. (2004) 'Global collective bargaining on Flag of Convenience shipping', *British Journal of Industrial Relations*, 42 (1): 47–67.

Lim, H. (2005) *The Social Clause: issues and challenges*. Geneva: ILO/ACTRAV.

Logue, J. (1980) *Toward a Theory of Trade Union Internationalism*. Gothenburg: University of Gothenburg.

Lorwin, L.L. (1953) *The International Labor Movement: History, Policies, Outlook*. New York: Harper & Brothers.

Lourenço-Lindell, I. (2002) *Walking the tight rope: informal livelihoods and social networks in a West African city*. Stockholm: Stockholm University.

Loveman, M. (1998) 'High risk collective action: defending human rights in Chile, Uruguay and Argentina', *American Journal of Sociology*, 104 (2): 477–525.

Lowell, B.L. (2007) *Trends in international migration and stocks, 1975–2005*. Social Employment and Migration working paper 58. Paris: OECD.

Lukes, S. (2002) *Power: A Radical View*. London: Palgrave MacMillan.

Margolies, K. (2008) 'Invisible no more: the role of training and education in increasing activism of Chinese healthcare workers in Local 1199 SEIU United Healthcare Workers East', *Labor Studies Journal*, 33: 81–92.

Martinez-Lucio, M. and Weston, S. (2004) 'European Works Councils—Structures and strategies in the New Europe', in Fitzgerald, I. and Stirling, J. (eds), *European Works Councils—pessimism of the intellect, optimism of the will*. London: Routledge: 34–47.

McIlroy, J. (2008) 'Ten years of New Labour: workplace learning, social partnership and union revitalization in Britain', *British Journal of Industrial Relations*, 46 (2): 283–313.

McShane, D. (1992) *International Labour and the Origins of the Cold War*. Oxford: Clarendon Press.

Miller, D. (2004) 'The limits and possibilities of European Works Councils in the context of globalisation', in Fitzgerald, I. and Stirling, J. (eds), *European Works Councils—pessimism of the intellect, optimism of the will*. London: Routledge: 198–210.

_____ (2005) 'Preparing for the Long Haul: Negotiating International Framework

Agreements in the Global Textile, Garment and Footwear Sector', *Global Social Policy*, 4 (2): 215–39.

Miller, D., Tully, B. and Fitzgerald, I. (2000) 'The politics of language and European works councils. Towards a research agenda', *European Journal of Industrial Relations*, 6 (3): 307–23.

Mondi (2007) *Annual reports and accounts 2007.* Gauteng: Mondi Group.

Moody, K. (1997) *Workers in a Lean World: Unions in the International Economy.* London: Verso.

Moon, S.S. (2006) 'Betwixt and Between Law and Practices: South Korean Women in the Workplace', *Asian Program Special Report*, 132: 6–13. http://www.wilsoncenter.org/topics/pubs/FinalPDF132.pdf (Accessed 15 August 2008).

Morgan, G. and Kristensen, P.H. (2006) 'The contested space of multinationals: varieties of institutionalism, varieties of capitalism', *Human Relations*, 59 (11): 1,467–90.

Mosley, L. and Uno, S. (2007) 'Racing to the bottom or climbing to the top? Economic globalization and collective labor rights', *Comparative Political Studies*, 40 (8): 923–48.

Munck, R. (ed.) (2004) *Labour and Globalisation: Results and Prospects*, Liverpool: Liverpool University Press.

Müller, T. and Rüb, S. (2002) 'Volkswagen and SKF: two routes to global works councils', *European Works Council Bulletin*, 42: 12–6.

_____ (2005) *Towards Internationalisation of Labour Relations?* Fachhochschule Fulda, Bonn: Friedrich Ebert Foundation.

N'Deba, L. and Hodges-Aeberhard, J. (1998) *HIV/AIDS and Employment.* Geneva: ILO.

Neuhaus, R. (1981) *International Trade Secretariats: Objectives, Organisation, Activities.* Bonn: Friedrich Ebert Stiftung.

Northrup, H.R. and Rowan, R.C. (1983a) *The International Transport Workers' Federation and Flag of Convenience Shipping.* Pennsylvania PA: Pennsylvania University Press.

_____ (1983b) *Multinational Collective Bargaining Attempts.* Pennsylvania PA: Pennsylvania University Press.

O'Brien, R. (2000) 'Workers and world order: the tentative transformation of the international union movement', *Review of International Studies*, 26: 533–55.

Odell, P.R. (1968) 'Oil and politics in Latin America', in Veliz, C. (ed.), *Latin America and the Caribbean: A Handbook.* London: Anthony Blond: 652–55.

Olmsted, M.S. (1959) *The Small Group.* New York: Random House.

Olson, M. (1965) *The Logic of Collective Action.* Cambridge MA: Harvard University Press.

Orhangazi, O. (2007) 'Financialization and Capital Accumulation in the non-Financial Corporate Sector: A theoretical and empirical investigation of the U.S. Economy: 1973–2003', *PERI Working Paper Series* 149. Amherst MASS: PERI, University of Massachusetts Amherst.

Otobo, A. (2007) 'Contemporary industrial relations in Nigeria', in Wood, G. and Brewster, C. (eds), *Industrial Relations in Africa.* Basingstoke: Palgrave: 162–81.

Oye, K.A. (1986) 'Explaining Cooperation under Anarchy: Hypotheses and Strategies' in

Oye, K.A. (ed.), *Cooperation Under Anarchy*. Princeton NJ: Princeton University Press.

Park, S. (1983) 'Japan', in Mielke, S., *Internationales Gewerkschafts Handbuch*. Opladen: Leske und Budrich: 621–43.

Pasture, P. (1999) *Histoire du syndicalisme chrétien international. La difficile recherche d'une troisième voie*. Paris: L'Harmattan.

Pasture, P. and Verberekmoes, J. (1998) 'Working-Class Internationalism and the Appeal of National Identity: Historical Dilemmas and Current Debates in Western Europe' in Pasture, P. and Verberekmoes, J. (eds), *Working-class internationalism and the appeal of national identity: historical debates and current perspectives*. Oxford: Oxford International Publishers.

Pearce, J. (2004) *Beyond the perimeter fence: oil and armed conflict in Casanare, Colombia*. Discussion paper 32. London: Centre for the Study of Global Governance, London School of Economics.

Rehfeldt, U. (1993) 'Les syndicats européens face à la transnationalisation des entreprises', *Le Mouvement Social*, janvier-mars: 69–94.

Reinalda, B. (ed.) (1997) *The international transport workers' federation 1914–1945: the Edo Fimmen Era*. Amsterdam: Stichting beheer IISG.

Reufter, W. and Rutters, P. (2002) 'International trade union organizations women's policy', *Economic and Industrial Democracy*, 23 (1): 35–58.

Robert, J.-L., Prost, A. and Wrigley, C. (2004) *The emergence of European trade unionism*. Aldershot: Ashgate.

Rogari, S. (2000) *Sindacati e impreditori: le relazioni industriale in Italia dalla caduta del Fascismo ad oggi*. Firenze: le Monnier.

Rossman, P. and Greenfield, G. (2006) *Financialization: new routes for profit, new challenges for trade unions*. Labor Education 1/2006, no. 142. Turin: ACTRAV.

Royle, A. (2005) 'The union recognition dispute at McDonald's Moscow food-processing plant', *Industrial Relations Journal*, 36 (4): 318–32.

——— (2006) *Working for McDonald's in Europe: the unequal struggle?* London: Taylor and Francis.

Rüb, S. (2004) *Can trade unions square up to the power of transnational companies?: Development of the global trade union network within the Nestlé corporation*. Bonn: Friedrich Ebert Foundation.

Ruggie, J.G. (1993) 'Multilateralism: The Anatomy of an Institution', in Ruggie, J.G. (ed.), *Multilateralism matters: The theory and praxis of an institutional form*. New York: Columbia University Press: 3–48.

——— (1998) *Constructing the World Polity: Essays on international institutionalization*. London: Routledge.

Rugman, A.M. (2001) 'The illusion of the global company', London: *Financial Times*, 6 January.

Russo, J. (1999) 'Strategic campaigns and international collective bargaining: the case of the IBT, FIET and Royal Ahold NV', *Labor Studies Journal*, 24: 23–37.

Rütters, P. (2001) "...I believe that I did just about the most I was capable of doing in this period with the means available..." – An Interview with Dan Gallin. Geneva: Global Labour Institute.

Schömann, I., Sobczak, A., Voss, E. and Wilke, P. (2008) *Codes of Conduct and International Framework Agreements: new forms of governance at company level.* Dublin: European Foundation for the Improvement of Living and Working Conditions.

Schwass, H. (2004) *Global Unions and their Regional Structures.* Bonn: Friedrich Ebert Foundation.

Sewell, W.H. (2008) 'The temporalities of capitalism', *Socio-Economic Review,* 6 (3): 517–37.

Silver, B. (2003) *Forces of Labour: Workers' Movements and Globalization since 1870.* Cambridge: Cambridge University Press.

Simon, H. (1983) *Organised labour against National Socialism: a case study of the International Transport Workers' Federation.* Unpublished MA dissertation, University of Warwick.

Singe, I. and Croucher, R. (2004) 'US Multinationals and the German Industrial Relations system', *Management Revue,* 16 (1): 123–37.

Snidal, D. (1986) 'The Game Theory of International Politics' in Oye, K.A. (ed.), *Cooperation Under Anarchy.* Princeton NJ: Princeton University Press.

Sogge, D. (2004) *Turning the problem around: FNV Mondiaal in Eastern Europe and the Soviet Union.* Amsterdam: Report for the Netherlands Ministry for Foreign Affairs and FNV Mondiaal.

Southall, R. (1995) *Imperialism or Solidarity: International Labour and South African Trade Unions.* Capetown: University of Capetown.

Spencer, B. (ed.) (2002) *Unions and Learning in a Global Economy: International and Comparative Perspectives.* Toronto: Thompson Educational Publishing.

Stiglitz, J. (2000) 'Democratic development as the fruits of labour'. Keynote address to the International Industrial Relations Congress, Boston, January.

Stone, R.W. (2004) 'The political economy of IMF lending in Africa', *American Political Science Review,* 98 (4): 577–92.

Taylor, M. (1987) *The possibility of cooperation.* Cambridge: Cambridge University Press.

Thelen, K. (2006) *How institutions evolve.* Cambridge: Cambridge University Press.

Theron, J. (2005) 'Employment is not what it used to be: the nature and impact of work re-structuring in South Africa', in von Holdt, K. and Webster, E. (eds), *Beyond the apartheid workplace: Studies in Transition.* Scottsville: University of Kwa Zulu Natal Press: 293–316.

Thomson, D. and Larson, R. (1978) *Where were you brother? An account of trade union imperialism.* London: War on Want.

Thorpe, V. and Mather, C. (2005) *ITGLWF 'Targeting Multinationals' Project Assessment.* Brussels: ITGLWF.

Tosstorff, R. (2004) *Die Rote Gewerkschaftsinternationale, 1920–1937.* Paderborn: Ferdinand Schoeningen.

_____ (2005) 'The international trade union movement and the founding of the International Labour Organization', *International Review of Social History*, 50 (3): 399–433.

Toye, R. (2003) 'The imperial preference system and the creation of the GATT', *English Historical Review*, 118 (478): 912–39.

Traub-Merz, R. and Eckl, J. (2007) International trade union movement: mergers and contradictions. Briefing paper 1. Bonn: Friedrich Ebert Foundation International Trade Union Co-Operation.

Tudyka, K.P. (1983) 'Internationaler Bund Freier Gewerkschaften', in Mielke, S. (ed.), *Internationales Gewerkschafts Handbuch*. Opladen: Leske und Budrich: 3–9.

Turner, T., D'Art, D. and Gunnigle, P. (2002) 'Multinational Corporations: A Challenge to European Trade Unions', *Irish Journal of Management*, 23 (1): 125–41.

UNCTAD (2008) *Development and Globalization: Facts and Figures*. New York: United Nations Conference on Trade and Development.

UNDP (2008) *Making the law work for everyone: Report of the Commission on Legal Empowerment of the Poor*. New York: United Nations Development Programme.

Upchurch, M. (2008) 'The organisation of work', in Muller-Camen, M., Croucher, R. and Leigh, S. (eds), *HRM: A case study approach*. London: CIPD publishing: 395–414.

Van der Linden, M. (2000) 'Conclusion: the past and future of international trade unionism', in Carew, A., Dreyfus, M., Van Goethem, G., Gumbrell-McCormick, R. and van der Linden, M. (eds), *The International Confederation of Free Trade Unions*. Berne: Peter Lang: 519–42.

Van Goethem, G. (2000) 'Conflicting interests: the International Federation of Trade Unions (1919–1945)', in Carew, A., Dreyfus, M., Van Goethem, G., Gumbrell-McCormick, R. and van der Linden, M. (eds), *The International Confederation of Free Trade Unions*. Berne: Peter Lang: 73–163.

_____ (2006) *The Amsterdam International: The world of the International Federation of Trade Unions 1913–1945*. Aldershot: Ashgate.

Verma, A. and Kochan, T.A. (eds) (2004) *Unions in the Twenty First Century: An international perspective*. London: Palgrave Macmillan.

Von Holdt, K. (2004) 'Political transition and the changing workplace order in a South African steelworks', in Webster, E. and von Holdt, K. (eds), *Beyond the Apartheid Workplace: Studies in Transition*. Scottsville: University of Kwa Zulu Natal Press: 45–72.

Von Holdt, K. and Webster, E. (eds) (2005) *Beyond the apartheid workplace: Studies in Transition*. Scottsville: University of Kwa Zulu Natal Press.

Vuckvic, M., Mistry, N., Beckmann, S., Lavollay, M. and Girrback, E. (2005) *Making Co-Investment a Reality: Strategies and Experience*. Geneva: GTZ/GBC.

War on Want (2007) *Anglo American: The alternative report*. London: War on Want.

Weait, M. (2007) *Intimacy and Responsibility: The Criminalisation of HIV Transmission*. London: Routledge Cavendish.

Wedin, Å. (1991) *La 'Solidaridad' sindical internacional y sus Victimas*. Estocolmo: Instituto de Estudios Latinoamericanos.

Weichselbaumer, D. and Winter-Ebner, R. (2003) 'A meta-analysis of the international gender pay gap', *Reihe Ökonomie*, Vienna: Institute for Advanced Studies: 135–55.

Western, B. (1997) *Between class and market: post-war unionization*. Princeton NJ: Princeton University Press.

Westney, D.E. (2008) 'Challenging the Trans National Model', *Socio-Economic Review*, 6 (2): 390–94.

White, A. (2006) *Making a World of Difference: Global Unions at Work*. Belgium: International Federation of Journalists.

Wick, I. (2004) *Workers' tool or PR ploy? A guide to codes of international labour practice*. Bonn: Friedrich Ebert Foundation.

Wilkins, M. (1974) *The making of multinational enterprise*. Cambridge MA: Harvard University Press.

Wills, J. (2002) 'Bargaining for the space to organise in the global economy: A review of the Accor-IUF union rights agreement', *Review of International Political Economy*, 9: 675–700.

———— (2004) 'Organising in the global economy: the Accor-IUF trade union rights agreement', in Fitzgerald, I. and Stirling, J. (eds), *European Works Councils—pessimism of the intellect, optimism of the will*. London: Routledge: 211–23.

Windmuller, J.P. (1954) *American labor and the International labor movement*. Ithaca NY: Cornell University Press.

Wood, G. and Brewster, C. (eds) (2007) *Industrial Relations in Africa*. Basingstoke: Palgrave.

Wood, G. and Frynas, J.G. (2006) 'The institutional basis of economic failure: anatomy of the segmented business system', *Socio-Economic Review*, 4 (2): 239–77.

World Bank (2007) *Global Economic Prospects 2007: managing the next wave of globalization*. Washington: World Bank.

Index